Tyranny of the Minority

How the Left is Destroying America

Ed Brodow

Tyranny of the Minority:
How the Left is Destroying America

© 2017 Ed Brodow
All Rights Reserved
ISBN: 978-1544614410

No part of this book may be reproduced, stored in a retrieval system, or transmitted by any means without the written permission of the author.

Published by Ed Brodow/ToutDroit Publishing
ed@brodow.com

Cover Design by Don Zirlilight
Photograph by Fran Wolterding

Books by Ed Brodow

In Lies We Trust
Negotiation Boot Camp
Beating the Success Trap
Fixer
Women from Venus
Negotiate with Confidence

Contents

Introduction: The Whole Enchilada	1
1. Obama's Legacy: A Nation Under Attack	3
2. Progressivism: The New Religion	27
3. Diversity: Divide and Conquer	44
4. Free Speech vs. Political Correctness	67
5. It's Not My Fault: Avoiding Personal Responsibility	81
6. Dismissing the Rule of Law	98
7. The Deep State: Unelected Bureaucracy	113
8. The Kafir's Dilemma: Sucking Up to Islam	126
9. A Culture of Lies	150
10. Black Hair and Campus Brainwashing	166
11. The Great Orange Hope	183
Recommended Reading	194
Acknowledgments	197
About the Author	198

"Better to be pissed off than pissed on."
US Marine Corps proverb

Introduction: The Whole Enchilada

We are engaged in an ideological war for the future of America. As Mark Levin said on his radio talk show, "We're fighting for the whole enchilada."

One faction in this war, known as the Right or conservative side, champions individual rights, freedom of speech, acceptance of personal responsibility, the US Constitution, and basic American values.

The other faction, known as the Left or progressive liberal side, militates for increased governmental control, limitations on free speech, replacement of capitalism with socialism, a reduction in American influence and affluence, and a dysfunctional version of social justice.

Social justice may sound like a good idea, but the Left's version is a naked grab for power by radical minority groups who claim to be oppressed by "racist white America." In a reversal of the civil rights revolution, this campaign is not in search of acceptance or equality. Their goal is to divide America so they can eventually trade places with their alleged oppressors. Hence the title, *Tyranny of the Minority*.

"Emphasis on group identities and group rights and progressives' clamoring for social justice will lead inexorably to a collectivist tyranny," says David Horowitz in *Big Agenda*. "This is a fight for American freedom—the soul of what this country stands for and the foundation of all its success."

As I gaze out on contemporary America, I see the ruthless indoctrination of our young people by left-leaning faculties at leading colleges and universities. I see the avalanche of "fake news" disseminated by biased media that have made a nest in the pocket of the Democratic Party. I see the demonization of conservatives, whites, and especially white men, who are defamed as racist, bigoted, sexist, misogynistic, and Islamophobic. I see the corrupt behavior of a professional class of politicians who benefit from illegal immigration and government encroachment on individual liberties.

The American Left and its senior partners, the Democratic Party and the mainstream media, are intent on destroying everything that is extraordinary about our country. *Tyranny of the Minority* attempts to explain how that destruction is taking place and the consequences of silent majority acquiescence. Many of the points I make are things you have been thinking but are afraid to say. If you are an American—whether you identify as conservative or liberal—my hope is that you will be engaged by the revelations in this book.

Ed Brodow
Monterey, Calif.

Chapter One
Obama's Legacy: A Nation Under Attack

Of all the books I read as a young student, and there were many, one that has maintained a firm grasp on my psyche is *Nineteen Eighty-Four* by George Orwell. I can still remember the ending when they torture Winston and he says, "Don't do it to me. Do it to Julia." Spare me, torture the one I love most in the world. Nothing in literature is so disturbing, I think, as this passage. Orwell's protagonist was turned into an empty shell by the totalitarian state that watched his every movement and even monitored his thoughts. In Winston's world, thinking was a crime. *Nineteen Eighty-Four* presaged political correctness.

Orwell had lived through the 1930s and the Second World War. He knew from personal experience how big government can trample all over individual rights. Orwell was particularly impressed by political strategist F.A. Hayek's statement that "collectivism gives to a tyrannical minority such powers as the Spanish Inquisitors never dreamed of." Orwell and Hayek believed that socialism "inevitably leads to despotism." They agreed that liberty and security were at opposite ends of the political spectrum. Big government, which makes a false promise of security, is capable of extinguishing liberty. Could that occur in the US?

"Totalitarianism," Orwell wrote, "if not fought against, could triumph anywhere." That's right, it could happen here. In fact, the Left has been working overtime to ensure that it does happen here. It was a bullet aimed at the heart of our republic during the eight years of the Obama administration.

Barack Hussein Obama presided over the first attempt by a sitting president to take America down. For eight years, I watched Obama's concentrated assault on our values. "He pledged to 'fundamentally transform America,'" wrote, Joseph Farah, editor of *WorldNetDaily*, "and he has done his level best to destroy it through fanning flames of hatred of all it stands for both inside the country and abroad." The worst part is how so many of my fellow Americans praised him for it.

Our country today is not the same one Obama took over in 2009. Showing his contempt for the Constitution, Obama did everything he could to expand the power of government at the expense of individual liberty. He ignored the separation of powers by doing an end run around Congress with his numerous executive orders. He pushed for increased entitlements, especially healthcare, because he knew they would increase government control over the individual. His statement, "If you've got a business—you didn't build that. Somebody else made that happen," invalidated the American Dream. Obama's positions in case after case denied the principle of personal responsibility, stoked the fires of racial discord, and made lawlessness acceptable. He attempted to move the country from meritocracy to an arbitrary system of race-based tests for "fairness" and "social justice."

Obama's foreign policy was designed to weaken us, embolden our enemies, and disappoint our friends. His desire to bring America down was clearly exposed by the shameful deal he made with Iran. We gave up everything, especially the economic sanctions that were putting maximum pressure on the mullahs, and in return we received... nothing. Iran is now guaranteed a clear path to obtaining nuclear weapons, placing the safety of the entire world in jeopardy—something that Obama swore would never happen.

With his disdain for private property (other people's, not his), Obama sought the redistribution of income and a transition from capitalism to socialism. He argued that the way to end poverty is to take wealth away from the rich. In fact, as Fox News analyst Monica Crowley explains in *What the (Bleep) Just Happened?* Obama wanted to redistribute everything that we have:

> "The leftists' grand design is centered on one basic premise: redistribute American power. Redistribute our wealth, economic energy, political strength, military power, cultural appeal, constitutional genius, and exceptional ingenuity both at home and abroad. Redistribute the elements of our greatness. Dilute our power in order to destroy it."

In other words, Obama attacked all the reasons why people from everywhere in the world want to live in the USA. *American Thinker* summed it up: "Barack Obama is trying to destroy America's essence, that commitment to liberty that makes her unique in this world, and that makes her uniquely American." From the first day of his presidency, Obama was apologizing all over the world for what he perceived as America's shortcomings and transgressions. At the core of Obama's message, said the *Heritage Foundation*, was "the concept that the US is a flawed nation that must seek redemption by apologizing for its past 'sins.'"

I still find it hard to believe that we are describing a president of the United States. "Never before in American history have we had a president who seeks decline," wrote Dinesh D'Souza in *Obama's America: Unmaking the American Dream*, "who is actually attempting to downsize his country. He subscribes to an ideology that says it is good for America to go down so that the rest of the world can come up." That ideology, according to D'Souza, is based on the belief that the colonization and rule by Western countries over the Third World are responsible for all the planet's ills. "Anti-colonialism is now embedded within Western liberalism," says D'Souza, "and you can learn its main principles at most leading colleges and universities."

A good question to ask is: Why would Obama want to destroy our country? His country. The answer can be found when we examine the list of prominent leftists whose ideological influence loomed large in Obama's personal development. His father was a radical, anti-colonial socialist in Kenya. Obama himself acknowledges that his primary influence from boyhood into young adulthood was Frank Marshall Davis, a card-carrying communist who hated the US and everything it represents. One of Obama's college mentors was Dr. John Drew, another communist agitator. At Harvard Law School, his mentor was Professor Charles Ogletree, a radical Marxist. After law school, Obama worked for groups founded by Saul Alinsky, a socialist community organizer who is known for his incendiary book, *Rules for Radicals* (see Chapter Nine). Obama's pastor for 20 years was Rev. Jeremiah Wright, the African-American rabble rouser infamous for screaming, "God Damn America!" Another notorious associate of Obama's was Bill Ayers, the radical-turned-professor who planned bombings for the left-wing terrorist organization known as the Weather Underground in the 1960s and 70s.

Obama always attempted to play down the influence of these vile gentlemen, of course with the adoring cooperation of the left-leaning media, but there is no doubt where his loyalties lie. With a similar pedigree, anyone else running for president would have been crucified by the press and the political class. Obama received a free pass.

The socialist Left, says Steve Baldwin in *Western Journalism*, believed the Obama era was the best opportunity ever to transform America to a socialist-based economy, and to eradicate our commitment to a Constitution designed to limit federal power. Their golden boy's eight-year-reign gave the Left an enormous head start. Obama's odious influence—even now—has the potential to dislocate 200-plus years of American excellence. The destructive forces set loose by eight years of his presidency have been implanted in our political system and in our brains. We need to root them out. Although these forces are hailed by the Left as "progressive," rejecting America's core values will eventually lead to the demise of the nation as we know it. We must clean up our act before the "shining city on the hill" is gone forever. Monica Crowley suggests that the failure to do so amounts to treason, that we are all "traitors to America for permitting our own government to seize our freedoms and move us into debilitating dependency with our own lazy acquiescence."

The election of Donald Trump was the first step in the right direction. He cherishes the values that Obama holds in contempt. Trump's motivation is his desire to "drain the swamp" in Washington and reaffirm a strong commitment to the foundational concepts of the Constitution. We need to give him our full support or Obama's legacy will turn the magnificent American experiment into something that is too abhorrent even to contemplate. It will not be a picnic. Obama's leftist supporters are doing everything possible to derail the Trump revolution.

What I have just described is sufficient to label Obama as the most reprehensible president in history—but his worst offense is the way he has acted as facilitator for the assault by special interest groups against the rights of the majority. I call this movement the *tyranny of the minority*. The majority has agonized and sweated and bled for those rights. We should be able to accommodate the rights of our minorities without depriving the majority of theirs.

By majority, I am referring to the people who work hard for their living, who pay taxes, who abide by the laws of the land, who make constructive contributions to society, and who encourage their children to take responsibility for themselves. I am especially referring to Caucasians of European descent, recent immigrants from East and South Asia, and any other persons from whatever background who hold the same values—because these are the people who have been responsible, and continue to be responsible, for most of the benefits that accrue to those of us who are lucky enough to live in this country. By giving them credit, I am in no way disparaging other peoples or ethnic groups. I am merely stating a fact. A fact that is not politically correct, but to hell with it—this book is responsible to facts, not to political correctness.

When I refer to minorities imposing their will on the majority, I am not referring to *all* blacks, *all* Hispanics, *all* women, etc. Most blacks, Hispanics, women, gays, etc., do not heed the siren call of the Left. I am referring to the radical, vocal minority within each of these minority groups, together with a cadre of white socialists. The minority within the minority. But make no mistake about this: The Left's agenda is driven by minority voices that have one thing in common. They hate America. They hate America because, as they perceive it, it is a nation where heterosexual, Christian, white males oppress everybody else. The size of the actual minority that constitutes the American Left is much smaller than the left-leaning media would like us to believe. Despite the size of this group, its harmful influence should not be underestimated.

Do as the Romans Do

The Egyptians. The Assyrians. The Persians. The Huns. The Mongols. The Turks. The First French Empire (Napoleon). The Third Reich (Hitler). The USSR. They prospered and then ... poof. Gone.

History supports this—all nations and empires enjoyed their day in the sun and then disappeared. No exceptions. The theory of "entropy" in physics backs this up on a theoretical level. It suggests that all matter in the universe is running down or decaying, and ultimately will be reduced to chaos. The universe, physicists tell us, has been decomposing from the original mass of matter (the "big bang") into smaller and smaller pieces that are moving further and further apart. The normal state of "things" is to go from something to nothing, not the other way around. It can be deduced from the theory of entropy that the social condition of human beings also must be in a state of decay.

The Roman Empire is a popular example of what can go wrong with successful cultures. It lasted almost 2,000 years if you include Constantinople. Quite impressive, but it still tiptoed off into the night. Many reasons have been advanced for Rome's demise: reliance of the army on mercenaries; government corruption; overexpansion; barbarian invasions; declining morals. Some scholars hold that Rome did not fall but evolved into a society with different values and institutions, i.e., the medieval world. No matter how you look at it, the coherent entity that was the Roman Empire ceased to exist.

The lesson of history is that it could, and probably will, happen to us. How do you suppose it will take place? It has been suggested that a democracy will implode when its citizens realize that they can vote themselves unlimited gifts from the public treasury. The majority will then vote for the politician who promises the most freebies. That sounds familiar. It sounds like the Democratic Party.

An Inside Job

If you wanted to destroy America from within, how would you do it? A good place to start is to attack its values. In order to imagine how our society might disintegrate completely or else evolve into a new entity with a different moral code, we need to identify the values that make ours a society worth fighting for. Then we need to recognize the forces that have the capacity to destroy those values.

A lot has been mentioned recently about "American exceptionalism." What is it? What is so wonderful about the USA? "Traditional American values are worthy of a passionate defense," says Monica Crowley. "American power is not something to be ashamed of but celebrated." Referring to these traditional values as "the American project," Charles Murray, author of *Coming Apart*, defines it as "the continuing effort, begun with the founding, to demonstrate that human beings can be left free as individuals and families to live their lives as they see fit, coming together voluntarily to solve their joint problems."

Here are the most enduring values of American culture, together with the forces from the Left that are waiting to destroy them:

1. The primacy of individual rights over unlimited governmental power

If you boil it down, what makes our society unique in

world history is the respect accorded the rights of the individual. This is a first in human development. Never before has respect for the individual been placed on a pedestal. No prior human society enjoyed as its core value the protection of individual rights. No prior human society took the trouble of writing it down in a single document. The US Constitution is designed to protect the individual from the power of external coercion. As the late Supreme Court Justice Antonin Scalia pointed out, the Constitution provides this protection by calling for the separation of powers and internal checks and balances. "The rights guaranteed by the US Constitution are not entitlements but *limits* to governmental power," says David Horowitz in *Big Agenda*. "It is these limits that guarantee individual liberty."

Before the Declaration of Independence, the individual served the society or the country in which he lived. What we consider "totalitarianism" was the norm. The state directed your life from birth to death. Along galloped the Founding Fathers as they affirmed "life, liberty, and the pursuit of happiness" by creating a republic designed to serve the individual and not the other way around. Political freedom, said F.A. Hayek in *The Road to Serfdom*, signifies "freedom from coercion, freedom from the arbitrary power of other men, release from the ties which left the individual no choice but obedience to the orders of a superior to whom he was attached."

We are at a dangerous moment in US history in which all that could be changing. The government has been trying to insinuate itself into every facet of our lives. "Every single one of [Obama's] initiatives," says *American Thinker*, was "directed at increasing government control in every area, with a corresponding decrease in individual liberty." Social mores are being torn apart. The press is no longer free to express contrary viewpoints. Universities are becoming "safe spaces" where only progressive liberal viewpoints are acceptable. Children are informing on their parents. The productive segment of the population is being demonized so "protected" classes can assert their entitlements.

An inverse relationship exists between size and scope of government, and respect for individual rights. Where there is more of one, there will be less of the other. As we allow the government to be responsible for more and more of our needs, we relinquish more and more of our independence. "It's a devils bargain," says Monica Crowley, "and the devil is running the show."

The American Left's ultimate alternative to democracy is socialism, where the government takes care of everything. Socialism is a form of big government that despises the individual and has been accompanied in every case by totalitarianism. Way back in 1848 Alexis de Toqueville wrote:

> *"Democracy extends the sphere of individual freedom; socialism restricts it. Democracy attaches all possible value to each man; socialism makes each man a mere agent, a mere number. Democracy and socialism have nothing in common but one word: equality. But notice the difference: While democracy seeks equality in liberty, socialism seeks equality in restraint and servitude."*

Socialism rejects private enterprise and private ownership of the means of production. "The entrepreneur working for profit," noted F.A. Hayek, "is replaced by a central planning body. If 'capitalism' means here a competitive system based on free disposal over private property, it is far more important to realize that only within this system is democracy possible. Where it becomes dominated by a collectivist creed, democracy will inevitably destroy itself."

2. Freedom of speech

All rights, including freedom of religion, stem from freedom of speech. Without freedom of speech, we have nothing. Zero. I can't emphasize this strongly enough. Free speech is regarded by the Left as an outdated concept. "People who defend and extol free speech," says Canadian psychologist Dr. Jordan Peterson, "tend to be branded as right-wingers." The concept known as political correctness, advocated by the Left, is a way of stifling free expression in favor of socially controlled thought. For some time, the Democratic Party has engaged in a campaign to destroy the First Amendment. The Democrats have attempted to silence anyone who denies global warming, criticizes Islamic terrorism, or advocates a stronger military.

Mark Steyn, author of *America Alone*, observed that we are turning into "one vast college campus" where there is one correct view and all others are prohibited. "The left says, we don't want to win the argument, we want to cancel the argument." The constitutional right to free speech amounts to nothing, Steyn believes, when public pressure kills dissent. He offers climate change as an example, where anyone who denies the Left's notion of global warming can be marginalized. "The pressure to conform in climate science is very real," says Steyn, "and the hostility to those who step out of line is extraordinary." This is the death knell of free speech.

For eight years under Obama, the US Government was busy enforcing the dictates of political correctness at the expense of unrestricted expression. A law was introduced in several states that would criminalize the denial of global warming. Loretta Lynch, Obama's attorney general, wanted to criminalize any criticism of Islam. I could wind up in jail for writing this book if California passes one of those statutes.

3. The rule of law

In Steven Spielberg's film, *Bridge of Spies*, Tom Hanks has a wonderful bit of dialogue. He tries to explain to a cynical CIA agent what it means to be an American. "I'm Irish and you're German," Hanks says. "But what makes us both Americans? Just one thing. One. Only one. The rule book. We call it the Constitution, and we agree to the rules, and that's what makes us Americans."

The US Constitution gives all of us a set of rules that we can depend on. It places limits on the ability of the government to wield coercive power against the individual. Government must be constrained by fixed rules that allow the individual to predict what the authorities will do in specific circumstances. The Constitution protects us. A critical example of legal protection is *habeus corpus*, which prevents the government from holding you indefinitely without showing cause. In America, we call this the rule of law.

By refusing to enforce a variety of laws, Obama contributed to an atmosphere of contempt for the rule of law. We are dealing with his failure right now as we debate the existence of sanctuary cities and the legality of Trump's Executive Orders on immigration. This is where the real significance of the US Constitution comes into play. Adherence to the Constitution precludes the possibility of a left-wing dictator who wants to impose arbitrary standards of justice. I feel certain that Obama would have enjoyed such a dictatorship with himself at the helm.

4. Separation of church and state

The Founding Fathers knew from personal experience and European history that merging politics and religion would lead to the destruction of the basic freedoms embodied in the First Amendment. Separating the two was a novel concept that made our country unique.

A dangerous part of the Left's agenda is bringing Islam and its ideology to our shores. One reason why Islam is incompatible with American values is that there is no separation of church and state in Islam. Shahi Hamid, author of *Islamic Exceptionalism: How the Struggle Over Islam is Reshaping the World*, explained in the *LA Times* that the difference between Christianity and Islam regarding the state has to do with each religion's central figure.

"Unlike Jesus, Muhammad was both prophet and politician. And more than just any politician, he was a state-builder as well as a head of state. Not only were the religious and political functions intertwined in the person of Muhammad, they were meant to be intertwined."

Pope Benedict XVI, in his book *Salt of the Earth*, argued that because of this important distinction, Islam cannot "be included in the free realm of a pluralistic society."

5. Social mobility

Historically, Europeans have been defined by class structure. Political economist Nicholas Eberstadt, writing in *Foreign Affairs*, suggests that rigid class systems in Europe led to the attitude that poverty was an accident of birth and that the poor were stuck in it. Even today, it is difficult for the average European to move up in life. I remember overhearing two French students in Paris lamenting the inflexibility of the French socio-economic caste system. "I'm thinking about moving to the US," one student confessed. "Over there, you can do whatever you want."

The American tradition is one of social mobility based on a system of merit. Andrew Carnegie worked for $1.20 per week at a cotton factory before he went on to amass one of the world's great fortunes. It is regarded as normal for Americans to move from one social class to another by starting their own business, changing jobs, obtaining more education, or marrying up.

Yet according to a paper published by the *Washington Center for Equitable Growth*, a left-leaning think tank, it is getting harder to move up in America. One reason given is increasing income inequality, a popular complaint by the Left that is used to divide Americans into warring political camps. The Left loves to condemn Americans who make a lot of money, suggesting that if one person gets richer another person must become poorer. Their view is that "America is zero-sum," says Monica Crowley. "Success in one place must be punished to elevate the less successful somewhere else." The Brookings Institution has blamed income inequality on "growing class-related gaps in family structure, parenting styles, school test scores, college attendance and graduation, and neighborhood conditions." This can be construed as a call for more entitlement programs that would increase the size of government, a leftist delight.

6. Private property

One of the differences between collectivist and capitalist economies is the right to private property that is inherent in the latter and absent from the former. Property rights include not only the legal ownership of specific property by individuals but also the ability to determine how that property is used. The Founding Fathers believed that private property rights are an essential component of individual rights. John Adams said:

> "The moment the idea is admitted into society that property is not as sacred as the law of God, and that there is not a force of law and public justice to protect it, anarchy and tyranny commence."

F.A. Hayek concurred in *The Road to Serfdom*:

> "The system of private property is the most important guarantee of freedom, not only for those who own property, but scarcely less for those who do not. It is only because the control of the means of production is divided among many people acting independently that nobody has complete power over us, that we as individuals can decide what to do with ourselves."

One of the ways in which the Left has encroached on private property rights is with the policy of eminent domain, the right of government to seize private property for public use. This practice has been subjected to abuse by the Left as it pushes for bigger government. As explained by Rep. Tom Reed in *The Hill*, the 2005 Supreme Court decision in *Kelo v. City of New London* expanded the government's right to impose eminent domain.

> "The Supreme Court held that 'economic development' constituted a 'public use' that justified the taking of private property through eminent domain. According

to this decision, the government can utilize eminent domain to seize your property whenever the government deems it necessary for 'economic development.'"

Justice Sandra Day O'Connor dissented, warning that, "Under the banner of economic development, all private property is vulnerable to being taken and transferred to another private owner." The *Kelo* decision, says Rep. Reed, is based on the leftist premise that big government is more capable of determining the best interests of citizens than the citizens themselves. It is "a chilling example," says Reed, "of the danger posed by government overreach and intrusion into the lives of American citizens."

An even bigger danger to property rights is posed by the UN. The unelected bureaucrats who run the UN are driven by what British political commentator Christopher Monckton refers to as a "totalitarian political ideology." German economist and UN official Ottmar Edenhofer admitted that the intent of the UN is to redistribute the world's resources under the aegis of a totalitarian world government. It means they want to take what you have and give it to people in the less developed parts of the world. The hysteria about climate change, warns Sen. James Inhofe, is fueled by the UN's desire for global control. That would play right into Obama's socialist dream of fundamentally transforming America.

"Property rights are the great equalizer—not of outcomes but of opportunity," Mark Levin wrote in *Ameritopia*. "This is the surest way to expand economic opportunity for the greatest number. Communism, and its socialist progeny, is tyranny. And it is tyranny without end since equality of economic outcomes is an illusion, requiring constant repression and plundering."

7. Equality of opportunity via free market competition

Respect for individual rights includes equality of opportunity. Not equality of outcome, a leftist goal which can never be accomplished without control by a coercive centralized authority. "A free society will not be one of equality," said James Peron, author of *Exploding Population Myths*. "Even if we were able to distribute all wealth equally, once the heavy hand of centralized control was removed, inequality would immediately result. The destruction of freedom is the only method for implementing equality of results."

Hand-in-hand with equality of opportunity goes unobstructed free market competition. A free market economy, says *Investopedia*, includes any and all voluntary economic activity and excludes control by "coercive central authorities." "The growth of civilization," said F.A. Hayek, "has been accompanied by a steady diminution of the sphere in which individual actions are bounded by fixed rules. The successful use of competition as the principle of social organization," Hayek wrote, "precludes certain types of coercive interference with economic life."

The more government intervenes in the free enterprise system, says economist Thomas Sowell, the worse everything will be for the country. "The first time the federal government intervened in the economy to get us out of a downturn was in 1930," says Sowell, "which means that for more than 150 years the federal government just stood by while the economy recovered on its own. In all that time there was never a depression as bad as the 1930s Depression where there was all kinds of intervention."

European economic life, says *The Economist*, is rife with "meddling governments" and the dictates of the European Union. But "Americans are supposed to be free to choose, for better or for worse. Yet for some time America has been straying from this ideal." In truth, we are catching up to Europe. Obama interfered with our system of competition by imposing more than 20,000 regulations that restricted the free market. Intrusive laws such as Dodds-Frank and Sarbanes-Oxley have made doing business in the US unbelievably complicated. Yet left-wing economists such as Paul Krugman continue to argue that it was deregulation that destabilized American economics and what we really need is even more control.

8. The "American Dream" and acceptance of personal responsibility

The myth of the rugged individual—self-reliance—holds that each person has the ability to succeed in life without the interference of government. It seems ironic today that a German immigrant wrote in 1825: "No country in the world has such a small number of persons supported at the public expense." Referring to this quality as *industriousness*, Charles Murray in *Coming Apart* describes it as "the bone-deep American assumption that life is to be spent getting ahead through hard work, making a better life for oneself and one's children." This is also known as the *American Dream*: Anyone can climb the ladder of success through hard work, determination, and a positive attitude. Murray emphasizes that "no other American quality" has so consistently fascinated the rest of the world.

Underlying this myth is the concept of assuming personal responsibility. Unlike the European idea that you are stuck with whatever condition you are born into, Americans believe that the individual has the power to determine his own fate. If you don't succeed, it is no one's fault but your own. You are ultimately responsible for whatever happens to you. "The cornerstone of a free society rests on the concept of the individual as a responsible self-determining agent," says Ilana Mercer in *Into the Cannibal's Pot*. "As long as this concept is under attack, free societies will be imperiled."

Nothing has contributed more to the success of America than the notion that each individual is capable of self-determination. "Self reliance remains the American way," says *Forbes Magazine*, "despite persistent messages that Americans need a strong helping hand from the state due to discrimination and life's other disadvantages."

The Left would like to kill the myth because they want everyone to become dependent on big government. Obama's ultimate goal, says Monica Crowley, was to "so weaken the middle class that it becomes utterly dependent on government." Obama's most un-American statement was, "If you've got a business—you didn't build that. Somebody else made that happen." In one quick blow, he invalidated the American Dream.

9. Adaptability

If Americans are known around the world for one personal attribute, it is our ability to adapt. One of my favorite World War II movies is *Gung Ho*, the rousing story of the Second Marine Raider Battalion in the assault on Japanese-held Makin Island. The colonel, played by a granite-jawed Randolph Scott, explains the mission to his men: "The principle weakness of the Japanese," he says, "is their inability to adapt to unusual situations." Not the Americans. We improvise. We overcome. We adapt.

The attitude of being flexible, accepting change, and discovering new ways to deal with challenges is an American characteristic. US corporations that don't change with the times usually wind up in the graveyard. Only 12% of the

Fortune 500 from 1955 are still around. Pan Am, Enron, PaineWebber, American Motors, and Woolworth's have been replaced by Amazon, Apple, Microsoft, Tesla, and Google. Our adaptability is responsible for the American entrepreneurial spirit.

We saw during the 2008 financial crisis that the Left would like to extinguish this entrepreneurial energy by enforcing government takeovers of the private sector. As reported in the *Washington Times*,

> "Mr. Obama touted the alleged success of his government-backed takeover of two-thirds of the domestic car business. 'The American auto industry has come roaring back,' he said. 'Now I want to do the same thing with manufacturing jobs, not just in the auto industry, but in every industry.'"

Obama was deliberately overstating the success of government takeovers. Once again, the push for big government lies behind the Left's strategy. And we know that big government and individual rights are not compatible.

Our system has been criticized, in some cases with good reason, for its shortcomings. As articulated by the "Founding Fathers," the right to "life, liberty, and the pursuit of happiness" was reserved for white men who owned property. The beauty of the Constitution, the answer to its critics, is its ability to reform itself. Eventually the promise of the Founding Fathers was extended to white men without property, then to African-American men, and then to women. After almost 250 years, the basic concept—respect for the individual—still works because of the system's inherent adaptability.

10. Patriotism

The unique circumstances that gave birth to the Declaration of Independence—in particular, respect for the rights of the individual—have fostered a spirit of patriotism that is one of the hallmarks of the American experience. For most of its history, the US has been the home of citizens who were willing to sacrifice their lives in service of their patriotism. As a former marine, I celebrate the service of many of my comrades who did exactly that.

Yet today we have a new challenge from the Left. Liberals are attempting to paint any and all manifestations of patriotism as expressions of hatred and bigotry.

Here is an example: Defending the globalist aspirations of the UN, actress Angelina Jolie warned that a "rising tide of nationalism" is "masquerading as patriotism." She hinted that Trump's refugee ban falls under this umbrella. Like many of her Hollywood buddies, Jolie thinks that Trump is a fascist for wanting to secure the borders.

This leftist argument was used by the Obama administration to justify its passivity in the face of real threats such as Islamic terrorism and illegal immigration. Any attempt by the government to fulfill its primary duty to protect us from external dangers is compared by the Left to fascism. Obama was a disciple of this train of thought. Trump, thankfully, is not.

"The left decided to rewrite history," says Ben Shapiro in *Bullies: How the Left's Culture of Fear and Intimidation Silences Americans*. "American patriotism had to be debunked. And so revisionist historians began portraying America as a nasty place, a colonialist land dedicated to the wiping out of brown and yellow peoples." America is portrayed by the Left as racist, militaristic, and misogynistic. As you will discover in Chapter Ten, this is the doctrine being taught at our colleges and universities.

Equal Time (well, maybe not equal)

Before going any further, I am a fair person and would like to acknowledge the point-of-view of the other side. Liberals see the problems facing America in very different terms. Economist Paul Krugman, conveniently waiving aside the destructive aspects of Obama's presidency, wrote an op/ed piece in the *New York Times* entitled "How Republics End":

> "Many people are reacting to the rise of Trumpism and nativist movements in Europe by reading history—specifically, the history of the 1930s. And they are right to do so. It takes willful blindness not to see the parallels between the rise of fascism and our current political nightmare. One thing all of this makes clear is that the sickness of American politics didn't begin with Donald Trump, any more than the sickness of the Roman Republic began with Caesar. The erosion of democratic foundations has been underway for decades, and there's no guarantee that we will ever be able to recover."

Krugman's worldview is the exact opposite of mine. He thinks Trump is Adolf Hitler. The weakness of his argument is exposed when he says, "The erosion of democratic foundations has been underway for decades." Is it possible that Krugman is unaware that we have had committed progressive liberals in the White House for 16 of the last 24 years? I see Obama and his leftist friends as the destructive force moving in the direction of totalitarianism, and Trump as the redeemer. The thesis of this book is that Krugman and his fellow progressives at the *Times* have been seduced by a dangerous value system that will take us down if unchecked. Author Neal Gabler, writing on Bill Moyers' website, seems to agree with Krugman. "America died on Nov. 8, 2016," Gabler alleges, "via electoral suicide." Oh, he's angry, this Gabler. "We the people chose a man who has shredded our values, our morals, our compassion, our tolerance, our decency, our sense of common purpose, our very identity— all the things that, however tenuously, made a nation out of a country." Fascinating how he comes to exactly the opposite conclusion that I do. I say that Obama shredded our values. This man believes Trump has done that. Of course, as a typical progressive liberal, he doesn't bother explaining to us exactly how Trump is destroying our values or even which values he is referring to. He simply assumes that you and I will agree with him, and so he is relieved of having to support his statement with good reasons. And here is the best part. Upon whom does Gabler place the blame? White people, naturally.

> "Disgruntled white Americans, full of self-righteous indignation, found a way to take back a country they felt they were entitled to and which they believed had been lost... Who knew that tens of millions of white men felt so emasculated by women and challenged by minorities? Who knew that after years of seeming progress on race and gender, tens of millions of white Americans lived in seething resentment, waiting for a demagogue to arrive who would legitimize their worst selves and channel them into political power?"

Once again we have the racist "white people are racist" argument that gained so much popularity during the Obama years. The purpose of this rhetoric is to divide the country so the Left can take over. Divide and conquer. But wait a minute? Stop the music. Wasn't it white people who elected the first black president? Calling America a white supremacist nation is absurd, says David Horowitz in *Big Agenda*, "since America—having just elected an African-American president twice—is arguably the most tolerant, least racist nation on earth." Liberals enjoy glossing over this inconvenient fact and too many conservatives let them get away with it.

Gabler also says that "objective, truthful journalism is dead, never to be revived." And guess who he blames for that. Donald Trump. Gabler believes it is Trump's fault that the media lie and deceive. He needs to read *In Lies We Trust* so he can appreciate that Trump has nothing to do with the mendacity of our fourth estate. Gabler no doubt blames Trump for the San Andreas fault, traffic jams in Midtown Manhattan, and hemorrhoids. I don't know what Gabler is putting in his coffee, but I'd like some. It might make it easier to swallow all this leftist propaganda.

Chapter Two
Progressivism: The New Religion

A friend of mine used to enjoy a charming 15-year-old tradition of spending Thanksgiving at his sister-in-law's. That tradition ended in 2016. The sister-in-law was a Hillary supporter. When she discovered that my friend's wife—her sister—voted for Trump, sister-in-law cancelled Thanksgiving. The same thing happened with another friend's niece and nephew. My friend invited both of them to his house for turkey. Niece declined because her brother voted for Trump and she could not stand to be in his presence. Two of my oldest friends have closed the Thanksgiving door on me because they are offended that I am a Trump supporter.

For the first time in my experience, something really vile is happening in our political discourse. Family is pitted against family. Friend against friend. We are witnessing a vicious intolerance by the Left of any and all conservative opinions.

If you supported Hillary Clinton, your conservative friends are willing to let it go. "Conservatives have allowed liberals to win the culture war because we're generally civil people," says Ben Shapiro in *Bullies*. "When the left says we're uncivil, we tend to shy away from the fight."

But if you supported Trump, your liberal friends—if you still have any—will vilify you in the most caustic way. Many liberals agree with actor Robert DeNiro's malicious and juvenile accusations against Trump and his supporters. In case you didn't hear about it, DeNiro called Trump "racist, dog, mutt, bozo, and pig," and that was just for starters. What a charming vocabulary he learned at the Actors Studio. The star of *Raging Bull* was so angry at the 2016 election results that he wanted to punch Trump in the face. Oh, didn't you know that every liberal is entitled to a temper tantrum? It is a fringe benefit that goes with membership in the Democratic Party.

Republicans and Democrats have never particularly liked each other, say sociologist Jonathan Haidt and author Greg Lukianoff, writing in *The Atlantic*, but their mutual dislike used to be surprisingly mild. Negative feelings have grown steadily stronger over the last 20 years. Political scientists call this process "affective partisan polarization." As each side increasingly demonizes the other, compromise becomes more difficult. Haidt and Lukianoff report that "implicit or unconscious biases are now at least as strong across political parties as they are across races."

Don't you find that frightening? I do. In 1996, Bill Clinton defeated Bob Dole with 49 percent of the popular vote and 379 electoral votes. If you supported the Republican, Dole, Clinton backers would still talk to you. Not anymore. The simple fact that you are conservative is enough to turn your liberal friends and family against you. For me, it all began with Obama. In 2008, when many acquaintances learned that I was not voting for their hero, they called me a racist. Why didn't I vote for Obama? I agreed with Thomas Sowell, a brilliant African-American who sees through the Obama facade: "This is a man who has actually accomplished nothing other than advancing his career through rhetoric," said

Sowell before the election. "It reminds me of a sophomore in college who thinks that he can run the world because he's never had to run anything." My liberal friends didn't care about my reasons. To them, no reason was good enough to justify my decision. One of my friends told me that I was a stupid racist and has never talked to me again. During and after the 2016 election, my Facebook feed was crawling with nasty, abusive statements charging that all Trump supporters are racists. Conservatives, by and large, don't behave like that.

Between Good and Evil

What accounts for this intolerant behavior by liberals? Throughout history, some human beings have used their religious beliefs to brutalize non-believers. The same Stone Age approach to conflict resolution that drives Islamic suicide bombers has wormed its way into the liberal playbook. Progressive liberals behave as though their ideology has been handed down from the mountaintop. Progressivism has morphed into our newest religion. With frightening similarities to Islam, the religion of the Left "is an authoritarian movement that wants total compliance with its dictates," says Daniel Greenfield, Journalism Fellow at the Freedom Center, "with severe punishments for those who disobey."

No longer regarded as merely a political contest, elections now represent a duel between good and evil. "Conservatives think liberals are stupid," said Fox News commentator Charles Krauthammer. "Liberals think conservatives are evil." You can tolerate stupidity but you can't countenance evil. When one half of the population perceives the other half as the devil, we are in big trouble. A belief system that is enshrined in a religion cannot tolerate criticism. (See Chapter Eight on Islam.)

In conformity with this new religion, a Hillary Clinton victory might have placed us closer to a political inquisition in which conservatives would be given the chance to confess and recant. In that scenario, unrepentant conservatives would be deported and replaced by Middle Eastern radicals. Is that so far-fetched? I don't think so. Not when millions of our friends are adopting a holier-than-thou attitude about how to run the country.

"You have to understand progressivism as a kind of religion—specifically, a fundamentalist religion," argues *The Federalist*. "In this view of the world, evil takes the form of any barrier to your self-expression." Classical liberals believed without reservation in free speech. Thanks to their religious fervor, contemporary liberals believe that freedom of speech is a flawed concept. Free speech should not apply to anything they disagree with, anything that contradicts their orthodoxy. Conservative viewpoints and some traditional religious beliefs are demonized by the Left as "hate speech." "People who violate the progressive code," says Mark Levin in *Liberty and Tyranny*, "are socially ostracized, sued for discrimination, forced to resign, and driven out of business."

Will the Real Fascist Please Stand Up

The movie projector in my mind keeps replaying a recent interview that I watched on Fox News. Judge Jeanine Pirro was being accosted by a cantankerous, middle-aged, African-American man who described himself as a communist. He was expressing his utter disdain for the election of Donald Trump. This man did not vote Republican because Trump, he says, is a fascist. Since he didn't vote for Trump, this man doesn't feel he is required to accept the result of the election...and he doesn't want you to accept it either. In fact, he wants you to act out your disapproval by doing everything you can to protest Trump and the fascism he represents.

"Are you an anarchist?" Pirro asked, getting right to the core of the matter as she always does. You could tell that she hit him where it hurts. Instead of answering the question, the man went from the ridiculous to the ultra-absurd, comparing Trump to Hitler. This interview is a perfect example of how the Left attempts to project its own fascistic tendencies onto the Right.

The way it works in this republic is, we have an election and the winner is the president for the next four years. When Obama was elected in 2008, I didn't like it but the voters had spoken and I knew I would have a chance to change it in 2012. Progressives don't feel they have to abide by this basic concept. Their agenda has been anointed with religious authority. Therefore they are entitled to subvert the entire process. That sounds to me like fascism.

Judge Pirro's interviewee is a classic contemporary liberal "progressive." He doesn't give a damn about your individual rights. He only cares about his own point-of-view, which he deems to be infinitely superior. Today's liberal will go on at length about "social justice" and the "common good," but his bottom line is a society that conforms to his ideological aims and his alone.

This aggravating man on Judge Pirro's TV show calls Trump a fascist, but in reality he is the fascist. Trump's political ideology is the diametrical opposite of fascism. Trump believes in the rights of the individual and the rule of law. Pirro's guest and his leftist buddies represent a palpable threat to our republic because they seek to destroy the very assumptions that make this country possible. They seek control over the individual. "Societal deconstruction and transformation are not possible," says Mark Levin in

Ameritopia, "if tens of millions of individuals are free to live their lives and pursue their interests without constant torment, coercion, and if necessary, repression. In America, breaking from the past means breaking the individual's spirit."

The ABCs of Statism

The Obama presidency encouraged left-wing extremists—like Pirro's guest—to come out of the closet in service of their new religion. What are the doctrines of this religion? In *Liberty and Tyranny*, Mark Levin refers to the new religion as *Statism*. He explains the beliefs of Barack Obama, a classic Statist. (As you read this quote, wherever the word "Statist" appears—think "Obama.")

> "The Statist urges Americans to view themselves through the lenses of those who resent and even hate them. He needs Americans to become less confident, to doubt their institutions, and to accept the status assigned to them by outsiders—as isolationists, invaders, occupiers, oppressors, and exploiters. The Statist wants Americans to see themselves as backward, foolishly holding to their quaint notions of individual liberty, private property, family, and faith, long diminished or jettisoned in other countries. They need to listen to the voices of condemnation from world capitals and self-appointed global watchdogs hostile to America's superior standard of living. America is said to be out of step and regressive, justifying the surrendering of its sovereignty through treaties and other arrangements that benefit the greater 'humanity.' And it would not hurt if America admitted its past transgressions, made reparations,

and accepted its fate as just another aging nation—one among many."

The progressive liberal, or Statist, does not see himself as an American. He is a citizen of the world, a globalist. Every positive accomplishment of the US is spun to appear as self-serving and anti-globalist. If Trump wants to protect the borders, for example, the progressive calls him a fascist. The weakness of this position, as Mark Levin points out, is that our enemies do not consider themselves to be world citizens. "They are not motivated by world opinion," says Levin, "but by their own desires. They seek strategic—economic and military—advantage." The progressive approach is a kind of turn-the-other-cheek response. It may work in a dream world, but certainly not in the real one we all live in. By turning the other cheek, as Obama did, we render the homeland unprotected as we become vulnerable to the political and military adventures of our enemies.

One of the key globalist arguments in favor of redistributing America's resources is the notion that we are only 5% of the world's population but we consume 25% of the world's energy. To liberals like Obama, this is unfair and immoral. They want the US to become poorer so the other 95% of the world can get richer—the same argument they use to advocate redistribution of wealth at home. Take money away from the rich so the poor will become less poor. The conservative, says Mark Levin, believes that (a) the US should not be penalized simply because we are more successful and productive than everybody else, and (b) one of the reasons we are more successful is that many countries are incapable of utilizing what resources they possess.

In addition to being an unabashed globalist, the progressive dislikes the US Constitution because it places limits on the scope of government. To reverse this important safeguard, progressives have gradually expanded the powers of the presidency to offset the built-in checks and balances. This trend goes all the way back to Andrew Jackson, but it really took off under Woodrow Wilson. He believed that a powerhouse state and a stronger executive branch were more desirable than respect for individual rights. In the 1930s it was FDR and the New Deal that lit a fire under the progressive engine. We can thank the New Deal for our bloated government and especially for the welfare state.

The progressive liberal looks forward to a socialist society that solves all human problems. The Left "substitutes glorious predictions and unachievable promises for knowledge, science, and reason, while laying claim to them all," writes Mark Levin in *Ameritopia*. The idealistic streak is epitomized today by Sen. Bernie Sanders. Referring to himself as a "democratic socialist," Bernie envisions a world "where poverty is absolutely unnecessary, where international relations are not based on greed ... but on cooperation ... where human beings can own the means of production and work together rather than having to work as semi-slaves to other people who can hire and fire." He thinks the US should emulate Denmark. "In Denmark," Bernie says, "there is a very different understanding of what 'freedom' means... they have gone a long way to ending the enormous anxieties that come with economic insecurity."

All Danish citizens have access to free health care, a generous pension, free college education, and a host of other goodies. But it all comes with a high price. In order to pay for these services, Danes are burdened with some of the highest taxes in the world and have little incentive to create and grow. They have exchanged liberty for security.

Nevertheless, Bernie Sanders wants:

1. Free college, which could cost taxpayers $70 billion

per annum.
2. A single-payer healthcare system that would replace private insurance companies with government programs and add $14 trillion to the national debt.
3. Massive wealth redistribution via tax increases and big-government programs.
4. A huge estate tax for Americans who inherit more than $3.5 million.
5. Curtailing of Constitutional free-speech protections.
6. Other expensive entitlements that go on forever.

Bernie's socialist agenda was realized in its entirety by Venezuela, a country that is rich in oil and that used to be one of the most prosperous in South America. Today it is a failed state—thanks to socialism. Yet this is where Bernie Sanders wants to take the US. Bernie brings to mind British philosopher C.S. Lewis, who said, "Of all tyrannies, a tyranny sincerely exercised for the good of its victims may be the most oppressive." I take comfort that, under President Trump, the ideological balance will swing back to a semblance of sanity—by which I mean respect for individual rights, the Constitution, and the rule of law.

White Privilege

The progressive liberal playbook includes several concepts that seek to increase the power of special interest groups over the majority: diversity, multiculturalism, white privilege, toxic masculinity, and social justice. With these seemingly innocuous words, the Left hopes to make the kind of radical changes that would give Barack Obama, Nancy Pelosi, and Chuck Schumer an orgasm. When I say the Left, in this case I mean a minority of Americans comprised of special interest groups—especially socialists, radical feminist women, and radical blacks, Hispanics, gays, and Muslims—all of whom have one thing in common: a big mouth. They are extremely vocal, they attract a lot of attention in the press, and they love to get in your face. And they have a common enemy: white people, and white males in particular.

On a prominent left-leaning TV talk show, a conservative guest was asked if she believed that white people could be the objects of racism. Her affirmative response was greeted with an onslaught of laughter, sarcasm, and derision. As I listened to her being reduced to a figure of foolishness by a leftist stooge, it occurred to me that not only are white people the objects of racism but we are at a point in our social history where traditional values are being turned upside down.

The Left has invented *white privilege*, a bigoted concept pointing to the unfairness of societal privileges that allegedly benefit all people identified as white. "The fact that white people are better off is not a privilege; it's earned," says David Horowitz, who wrote *Black Skin Privilege and the American Dream*. Not all racial disparities are inherently racist, he says. "If racial disparities prove discrimination, then the National Basketball Association is racist. Probably 90 percent of its players are black." It's not white privilege that's preventing blacks from doing better, Horowitz argues. It's their behavior, such as the propensity to commit violent crimes and the inability to build more intact families.

Despite the rhetoric, the white privilege argument is a racist attack on white people. "White people are the only group in the country that is discriminated against via Affirmative Action by official government policy," wrote John Hawkins at *Townhall.com*. Look at the headlines:

Obama's Lackey Tells Students "There Are Too Many Whites In Top Government jobs."

College Celebrates People Who Want To "Breed White People Out Of Existence"

Teacher: Minorities Don't Have to Show Up or Hand in Assignments on Time Because of "White Privilege"

A public school in Los Angeles has been denied funding because its enrollment is composed of too many white students. School systems across the country, according to Bill O'Reilly on Fox's *O'Reilly Factor*, are recommending that teachers should treat minority students differently than whites, that black students should not be disciplined for a variety of behavioral offenses because the responsibility for those behaviors lies with the white community. Therein lies the danger of the white privilege argument. Buying into the notion of white privilege compounds an existing problem that is destroying our minority communities. Affirming white privilege is an attempt by non-whites to avoid taking personal responsibility. The assumption that minorities are falling behind because white people have the deck stacked in their favor is self-defeating and irresponsible. "By allowing minority kids to avoid responsibility," says O'Reilly, "the school districts are dooming many of them to a life of poverty and chaos."

The conclusion of the philosophy is that blacks deserve preferential treatment in order to counterbalance the effects of white privilege. It is affirmative action on steroids. Affirmative action has a divisive effect on society. "Far and away the most egregious form of government interference with the contractual rights of private persons and organizations is carried out in the name of affirmative action," says Richard Pipes in *Property and Freedom*. "Initially conceived as a means of enforcing principles of nondiscrimination in regard to black citizens... [affirmative action] was soon extended to other groups and ultimately turned into a vehicle for reverse discrimination against whites and males."

Nor does it do justice to the intended beneficiaries. Affirmative action recipients at colleges and universities experience a high dropout rate. *Mismatch theory* describes minority students who are accepted at schools beyond their aptitude, creating a sense of failure, depression, and alienation. At UCLA, they had to create a collection of useless majors such as Critical Race Theory and Black Studies in order to make it easier for affirmative action students to survive. David Sacks and Peter Thiel, authors of *The Diversity Myth*, point out that "a racist past cannot be undone through more racism. Race-conscious programs and the heightened racial sensitivity they cause is a source of acrimony and tension instead of healing." To protect individual freedoms, says Ilana Mercer, we must avoid separating people from their rightful revenues in the name of affirmative action. "This entails recognizing [affirmative action] for the codified and legalized theft and coercion it really is."

Unfortunately, the message the Left wants to send to African-Americans is: "You are not smart enough or capable enough to compete, so we will give you welfare payments, food stamps, Medicaid, free cellphones, and affirmative action." The result of all these government programs has been to reinforce an underclass that is dependent upon government handouts and, thus, big government. The Left is all for it.

Even more counter-productive than affirmative action is the demand for reparations. The implication is that descendants of slaves deserve some form of compensatory payment. There are three main arguments against making reparations: (1) it would have a destructive effect on the black community; (2) it is not fair; and (3) it is racist.

First, the effect of more free money flowing into the African-American community would only exacerbate the problem of failure to accept personal responsibility. Reparation payments would reinforce the victim mentality and further discourage blacks from taking the necessary steps to improve their lot in life. Second, reparations are about as unfair as it can get. My family, for example, did not reside in the US during the period of slavery. Is it fair to demand that I owe a monetary penalty to compensate for something the Brodow family had nothing to do with? And even if the Brodows were here prior to 1865, and even if they did own slaves, it would not justify payment of a penalty because all the people who were involved in slavery are long dead and gone. No living blacks experienced slavery and no living non-blacks ever owned slaves. A century and a half have transpired since the end of the Civil War—slavery comes under the heading of ancient history. It is racist to elevate one race at the expense of all others. It could lead to demands for reparations from descendants of Irish, Italian, and Jewish Americans based on institutional discrimination experienced by their ancestors. But if we accept the racist notion that "black lives matter," rationality goes out the window and the Left will not be stopped by sensible arguments.

The Left is also in favor of lowering the percentage of white people. No kidding. By mid-century, whites are expected to be a minority in the US. Listen to Edward J. Erler, political science professor and co-author of *The Founders on Citizenship and Immigration*:

> "It is now widely recognized that the Immigration Act of 1965 was intentionally designed to alter the racial and ethnic mix of the population of America. It has

> been an overwhelming success; demographers predict that by 2040 whites of European descent will no longer be a majority, having been displaced by people of Asian, African, Latin American, and Hispanic descent."

And Ilana Mercer adds:

> "The consequence of the mass importation of poor, Third World immigrants is that minorities intractably hostile to the host culture are on their way to consolidating a permanent majority. The Democratic Party is this nascent majority's political organ, offering a platform of preferential policies for a voting bloc whose interests are viewed through the prism of racial affiliations."

It is one thing to predict that whites will no longer be the majority, but to "celebrate" it, to be excited about it, to advocate for it, is definitely racist and anti-white. The Left celebrates this demographic shift on the assumption that most non-white people will vote Democratic. If most immigrants voted Republican, it has been suggested, Congress would have resolved the immigration crisis years ago.

Toxic Masculinity

Being white is only part of the perceived problem. The Left is now sending me the message that it is high time I apologized not merely for my white privilege but also for my *toxic masculinity*. (Is someone putting me on, or did they mix LSD in with my flu shot?) Up to now, Western culture has been dominated by white males. "We live in the strongest, most powerful, most prosperous nation in human history," said John Hawkins, "and if we're being honest, white men probably deserve 95% of the credit for that." The Left wants to take all the credit away.

To a large segment of the left-leaning population, white men are the enemy. Feminine attributes are being placed on a pedestal while progressive women refer to men as "homo obnoxious." Todd Starnes observed on *Fox News* that "in the hit Broadway musical, *My Fair Lady,* Professor Henry Higgins laments in a song, 'Why can't a woman be more like a man?' Today," says Starnes, "Professor Higgins might be singing a different tune, 'Why can't a man be more like a woman?'"

In order to deter toxic masculinity, many colleges have "opted to condemn manliness," says *Forbes*. Brown University, for example, has a program titled "Masculinity 101" where male students can unlearn their toxic masculinity. Oregon State University unveiled a conference where students will "engage in collective imagining to construct new futures for masculinities, unrestricted by power, privilege, and oppression." Duke University has a similar project sponsored by—you guessed it—the Women's Center.

"A group of academics telling boys not to be men," says *Forbes* in a moment of sanity, "will only make the problems associated with young men who haven't learned to be gentlemen worse."

Toxic masculinity is being used as a way of getting even by radical feminists. In a shocking case that just hit the airwaves, Bill O'Reilly of the *O'Reilly Factor*—the most popular figure on cable news—was fired from Fox News after a series of accusations of sexual harassment. None of them has been litigated although several suits are alleged to have been settled. The latest charge of toxic masculinity was from a woman who claimed that O'Reilly promised to take her to dinner and then reneged. He also is alleged to have advised the woman to show more cleavage. Another woman accused him of referring to her as "hot chocolate." O'Reilly may be guilty of crass behavior, but that does not provide the basis for a law suit. Rather than adding up to a convincing case, it sounds more like a witch hunt. O'Reilly has denied the truth of all charges. In the absence of concrete evidence, I can only conclude that he is no more guilty of sexual harassment than Donald Trump after the latter made some silly off-the-record comments about consensual sex with women. Both of them were convicted in the courts of political correctness and male bashing. Trump managed to survive the attack because the voters didn't buy it. O'Reilly, as a conservative caught in the crosshairs of the liberal-controlled media and feminist rage, was not so lucky.

Unfortunately, we have reached a place in our political history where the strategy of the Left is to launch personal attacks against right-wing adversaries. We have reached a place in our social history where witch hunts are a regular feature and public figures can be brought down by malicious rumors. With its presumption of guilt, toxic masculinity will make successful men vulnerable to false charges of sexual harassment by opportunistic women who are encouraged to bring suit by unethical attorneys.

The Left will shout me down if I say that most of the white men I know work hard in order to fulfill their potential. They will remind me that 98% of mass murderers are men. That men are hairy beasts. If you are foolish enough to believe in traditional masculinity, you run the risk of being called sexist, racist, fascist, Nazi, or worse (if that is possible). Frankly, I am sick of all this self-serving propaganda. I'm tired of being told how dysfunctional I am by people who can barely use toilet paper. In the same way that white privilege is racist, toxic masculinity is sexist.

Men are being marginalized at every opportunity. They are being taught that they are worthless. They are being denied opportunities reserved for minorities and women. It is not about equality for the sexes. It is about special privileges for women, who are now regarded as a victimized minority group. Women no longer seek equality, they want to be "more equal." Don't know what I mean? Read the next chapter and you will find out.

Chapter Three
Diversity: Divide and Conquer

Now we come to the Left's favorite construct, *diversity*. "Sometimes," said Thomas Sowell, "it seems as if *diversity* is going to replace *the* as the most often used word in the English language." The dictionary definition of diversity is the political and social policy of encouraging tolerance for people of different backgrounds. On the surface, it sounds terrific. Tolerance is always a laudable ideal. Unfortunately, the Left has distorted its meaning. To progressives, diversity means that we must give special privileges to certain protected classes of people. The special classes are composed of minorities such as blacks, Hispanics, and gays. For some reason, women have been designated as a special class even though they represent a majority of the population. Diversity means that minorities get control over the system at the expense of the majority, which happens to be white.

While Asians are considered a special class due to their small numbers, they usually get lumped in with whites. Many Asians and whites share the same strong work ethic and respect for education. It has been suggested that the economic success of Asians in America has worked to their disadvantage. They are the big academic achievers of this generation, yet admission to colleges and universities is regularly denied to Asian applicants in favor of less qualified students from more vocal groups, i.e., blacks and Hispanics. Meritocracy has been superseded by diversity.

Another small group that has paid a price for their economic success is Jews. In spite of a dramatic uptick in anti-Semitic incidents throughout the US, Muslims are considered a protected class but Jews are not. Campus anti-Semitism has become a frightening trend that is an offshoot of the diversity movement.

Diversity implies intolerance of Caucasians. Minority groups are said to need protection because of the allegation that they are oppressed by the white majority. According special privileges to minorities is the Left's way of making white people into a minority. The Left's version of diversity attempts to divide Americans between oppressors—heterosexual, white, Christian males—and victimized groups of minorities and women. "It is the old Marxist wine in new bottles," says David Horowitz in *Big Agenda*, "and the results are bound to be similar."

Protected classes are entitled to many special perks: they receive academic privileges (special courses on feminism, black studies, Latino studies, gay studies); they are often allowed to get away with breaking the law; they are the beneficiaries of affirmative action and quotas. Meritocracy and diversity are opposites. Merit has always been prized in America. Now skin color outranks merit. However, you don't get any points if your skin color is white. Progressives, says Horowitz, are using a politically correct term—*people of color*—to "further isolate the white European American majority as an oppressor of everyone else." Diversity is presented as a remedy for intolerance but all it does is increase racism by dividing the population into hostile groups.

A classic example of diversity policy relates to admission

standards at colleges and universities. Those clamoring for diversity argue that black and Hispanic students must be given preference because they do not have equal access to universities, and thus are "underrepresented." That claim is false when black and Hispanic students are judged by the same standards applied to other students. The problem is confusion between access and performance. "Access is not the issue," explains Thomas Sowell. "Performance is the issue. I have had as much access to a career in professional basketball as Michael Jordan had. He just happened to play the game a lot better." If minorities are underrepresented in colleges and universities, it is the fault of inadequate secondary school preparation—not the standards demanded by colleges and universities.

The Left would like to see our standards lowered across the board, which would "level the playing field" and reduce our competitiveness in the world. Should we seek social justice by lowering the standards to the lowest denominator via affirmative action, or should we require the lowest denominator—in this case, minority students—to meet the higher standard? Lowering standards has given us an educational system that is producing substandard results. Statistics that show the US lagging behind in educational accomplishments are proof that the Left is succeeding. So why are thousands of university administrators collaborating with the radical students instead of standing up for higher standards? We need more college administrators like Oklahoma Wesleyan University President Dr. Everett Piper, who told students, "This is not a daycare. This is a university!"

Ironically, where you have obedience to diversity, there is no diversity of thought. People who demand attention to diversity are really against viewpoint diversity, also known as free speech. Diversity means "it is great to look different as long as you think the way I do." When universities diversify their faculties, the result usually is the suppression of the conservative point-of-view. Whatever you say that disagrees with the leftist ideology is *hate speech*. Today's colleges and universities "are only diverse in terms of identity. In terms of ideology, they are all but homogeneous," said William Deresiewicz, author of *Excellent Sheep*. "You don't have 'different voices' on campus, as these institutions like to boast; you have different bodies, speaking with the same voice." Thomas Sowell agrees. Diversity of thought is no more welcome on college campuses, he says, "than it has been under the Taliban in Afghanistan." (see Chapter Ten)

When you look behind the curtain, diversity is discriminatory. This is the tyranny of the minority at its most virulent. "Diversity in today's America," says Scott Greer in *No Campus for White Men*, "simply means having fewer whites around." The basis for diversity policy is that certain groups are encouraged to identify themselves as victims. (See Chapter Five for a discussion of the victim mentality.) According to Thomas Sowell, some people say, "I am a victim. Therefore, if you do not give in to my demands and let me walk over you like a doormat, it shows that you are a hate-filled, evil person."

Why the Left Loves Diversity

Diversity has several uses for the Left. First, Many corporations have created whole departments to train their employees in the virtues of diversity. This increases the cost of doing business, again playing into the liberal scheme of weakening America, and it has created jobs for people who otherwise would be unemployable—a subtle form of welfare. Second, diversity exploits past grievances to extort wealth from the productive segments of society. As I continue to point out, redistribution of resources is one of the Left's primary goals. Finally, and most significantly, diversity creates division and hatred. Instead of making everyone feel they are part of a unified American social structure, diversity plays into the leftist strategy of "divide and conquer." With its emphasis on diversity, says Mark Levin in *Ameritopia*, the Left achieves the "balkanization" of society. It exploits discontented elements and invalidates the individual:

> "It assigns him a group identity based on race, ethnicity, age, gender, income, etc., to highlight differences within the masses. It then exacerbates old rivalries and disputes or it incites new ones. This way it can speak to the well-being of 'the people' as a whole while dividing them against themselves, thereby stampeding them in one direction or another as necessary to collapse the existing society or rule over the new one."

Rep. Mo Brooks explains diversity in terms of vote-getting:

> "It's a part of the Democratic Party's campaign strategy to divide Americans based on skin pigmentation and to try to collect the votes of everybody who is a non-white on the basis that whites are discriminatory and the reason you are where you are in the economic ladder is because of racism."

Diversity has given birth to divisive groups such as Black Lives Matter and La Raza. The Left's version of diversity means the opposite of the traditional motto of the United States, "E pluribus unum." Out of many, one. Wherever you came from, whatever you were, you are American now. The Left wants it to read, "Out of one, many." For the Left, the whole purpose of diversity is division. For the rest of us, "It has not been our diversity," said Thomas Sowell, "but our ability to overcome the problems inherent in diversity, and to act together as Americans, that has been our strength."

Diversity and *multiculturalism* are cousins. Where diversity is about individual differences such as national origin, race, gender, or religion, multiculturalism has to do with the difference between cultures. Multiculturalism infers support for the presence of several distinct cultural or ethnic groups within a society. The promise of multiculturalism is that it may provide the antidote to racial, social, and other tensions in the US. In reality, "the multiculture exists to destroy Western culture," say David Sacks and Peter Thiel in *The Diversity Myth*. No one knows precisely what multiculturalism means and so it is easily susceptible to misinterpretation. Although colleges and universities have used multiculturalism as an excuse to diversify their student bodies, according to Sacks and Thiel, their real intention is to impose intellectual conformity. "Speech restrictions, political grading, ostracism of nonconformists, unqualified denunciations of the West, and a curricular obsession with oppression theory and victimology make clear that toleration of dissenting viewpoints is not a multicultural virtue." Students, Sacks and Thiel suggest, may "resemble the bar scene from *Star Wars*" but in reality they are "like-minded activists."

The best argument against multiculturalism in the US is that America has always been "anticultural." Each group of immigrants gradually shed its foreign identity as it was assimilated into the US. The Irish and Italians and Koreans did not meld their cultural identities together, as suggested by the "melting pot" metaphor. "America represented an opportunity to break with the cultures of their pasts and to forge their own destinies in the New World," Sacks and Thiel conclude. "For better and for worse, the rejection of culture has been carried further than anywhere else in history." Instead of defining themselves by cultural characteristics, Americans define themselves in terms of the values enumerated in Chapter One: respect for the individual, freedom of speech, property rights, and so on. In Chapter Ten, I will describe how diversity and multiculturalism are leftist tools for creating dissension on campus.

Multiculturalism has become a popular concept in European countries that have deliberately opened their doors to a tidal wave of ethnic immigration, especially from the Middle East. As I will explain in Chapter Eight, this experiment has placed many European countries on the brink of civil war. The American Left would be delighted to see the same thing happen here. Monica Crowley calls this inciting class warfare:

> "Immigrant populations, both legal and illegal, have been allowed to siphon themselves off from American culture, often resulting in mini-nations within the larger one. They have been aided and abetted by the leftists, who have encouraged foreigners to remain foreign, have supplied them with grievances against America, and have tried to make America conform to them instead of the other way around. The basics of the [liberal] playbook—grievance identification and multicultural celebration—are now applied routinely in our schools and universities. The result has been an America that is divided against itself."

A related concept is *cultural relativism*, the view that all beliefs, customs, and ethics are morally equivalent. What is considered immoral in one society may be considered moral in another, and, since no universal standard of morality exists, no one has the right to judge another society's customs. So if Muslims want to throw gays off of rooftops, who are we to criticize? Thomas Sowell and Mark Steyn have argued against the idea that all cultures are equal. Barack Obama would undoubtedly disagree with them. During my research on the Internet, I found this candid statement by an anonymous contributor that sheds some light on the subject:

> *"There's a reason why the dominant culture in the United States is a white, European culture: it was founded by white Europeans, following systems of thought and law that were distinctly European in origin; in other words, because that culture actually works. If it were any different, then we'd be the Third-World shithole and Zimbabwe or Laos would be the most powerful country on Earth. Therefore, the concepts of Diversity and Multiculturalism, pushed passed a certain limit, are a complete waste of time and energy that can achieve no practical good, and do little more than degrade a successful culture and sap the morale of those who live in it."*

Former Colorado Governor Richard D. Lamm has an interesting tongue-in-cheek formula that sends up the Left's emphasis on diversity:

1. "Encourage all immigrants to keep their own language and culture. Replace the melting pot metaphor with the salad bowl metaphor. Ensure that we have various cultural subgroups living in America enforcing their differences rather than as Americans, emphasizing their similarities."
2. "Make it taboo to talk about anything against the cult of diversity."

3. "Make it impossible to enforce our immigration laws. I would develop a mantra: That because immigration has been good for America, it must always be good. I would make every individual immigrant symmetric and ignore the cumulative impact of millions of them."

In one of the most humorous take-downs of diversity, Mark Steyn tells the story of a woman at Wellesley College in Massachusetts who identified as a man. She was denied a role in the student multicultural apparatus because they said she was now a white male and therefore insufficiently diverse to be a diversity officer. "She diversified herself out of the diversity business," says Steyn, "and into the white male business."

Social Justice

Talk of diversity usually leads to a discussion of *social justice*. The surface meaning of the term social justice suggests that everyone should be treated with fairness and equality. But as with diversity, the meaning of social justice has been perverted by the Left. According to *The Heritage Foundation*, the term social justice "has been bent by secular 'progressive' thinkers to mean uniform state distribution of society's advantages and disadvantages." In other words, equality of outcome. "Social justice entails a 'redistribution' of resources," says the *American Sociological Review*, "from those who have 'unjustly' gained them to those who justly deserve them." The paradox of social justice is that in theory it aims for diversity, but in reality it enforces sameness.

"The demand for 'social justice,'" says Ilana Mercer, "becomes a demand for redistribution and revenge. Ultimately, egalitarianism is inimical to liberty. We must learn to live with and accept enduring and important differences between individuals and groups."

Social justice means that minorities don't have to listen to reason because reason is the creation of white people, who are full of crap by virtue of their white privilege. Social justice is opposed to reason. Social justice is opposed to viewpoint diversity.

When discussing social justice, it is customary to discuss the *common good*. The difficult question is who decides what is the common good? F.A. Hayek suggests that the notion of common good is meaningless as it "only conceals the absence of real agreement on the ends of planning." In practice, what happens is "the common good becomes an excuse for total state control," argues *The Heritage Foundation*. "That was the excuse on which totalitarianism is built. You can achieve the common good better if there is a total authority, and you must then limit the desires and wishfulness of individuals." David Horowitz echoes this sentiment in *Big Agenda* when he says that social justice amounts to a war on individual rights.

And so we are back to the desire of the Left to suppress individual rights and redistribute wealth. Daniel Greenfield of the Freedom Center explains the choice we face:

> *"We can have a system of government based around the Constitution with democratically elected representatives. Or we can have one based on the ideological principles of the left in which all laws and processes, including elections and the Constitution, are fig leaves for enforcing social justice. But we cannot have both."*

Identity Politics vs. the Civil Rights Movement

What is the real driving force behind the push for

diversity and social justice? Is it a campaign for equality? My thesis is that minority special interest groups are using the banners of "equality," "diversity," and "social justice" as a power grab. The intention is to impose their agendas on the majority with no regard for fairness or the democratic process. It is a fight for equality only in the Orwellian sense. "All animals are equal," George Orwell wrote in *Animal Farm*, "but some animals are more equal than others." What we are observing is really a grab for power by vocal minority groups—especially radical elements among feminist women, blacks, Latinos, gays, and Muslims—who want to be more equal than others.

"This is where victims turn into perpetrators," says Ben Shapiro in *Bullies*. Where civil rights leaders once called for equal rights, now they call for special rights. "The grand rhetoric of diversity," political commentator Michelle Malkin wrote in *Townhall*, "masks the true intent: solidifying the power of the few over the many." Minority special interests are attempting to convince the white majority that it should submit to the minority will.

When Dr. Martin Luther King said, "I have a dream," he was dreaming of a colorblind America. He was dreaming of equality. "I have a dream," he said, "that my four little children will one day live in a nation where *they will not be judged by the color of their skin*, but by the content of their character." A beautiful sentiment with a vision for an inclusive country. That is what the Civil Rights Movement was all about. People gave their lives in service of the most significant peacetime event of the 20th Century. The Left's campaign for diversity is destroying everything those people fought for on the streets of Selma. The minority special interests are not seeking equality. When the Left advocates diversity, they want people to be judged by the color of their skin. In a multicultural world, character becomes irrelevant as the Left divides Americans into competing groups based on color and ethnicity. When you have these groups at each other's throats, the only possible objective is power. Make no mistake about it, our special interest groups are seeking control—period. The battle will determine which group will be "more equal." If Dr. King were alive today, he would be the first to recognize that African-Americans are likely to suffer most as a result of this perversion of his dream.

Welcome to *identity politics*, where you take sides based on your race, religion, sex, ethnicity, social background, etc., instead of taking sides based on substantive political viewpoints. You are judged based on the group you belong to, not on your ideological or political preference. The American value of respect for the individual is replaced by tribalism. The Huns are at the gates of Rome once again. Identity politics and its goal of social justice are radical departures from America's social contract, says David Horowitz. By empowering groups instead of individuals, they are antithetical to American principles proclaiming that individuals have inalienable rights that government cannot take away.

> *"The civil rights revolution should have put an end to government-imposed racial categories that privileged some groups over others and deprived individuals of their right to equal treatment under the law,"* said David Horowitz. *"But Democrats have spent the last 50 years reintroducing racial categories into virtually every aspect of public life and creating bureaucracies to enforce race-based privileges for designated groups."*

All of this moralizing and carrying on in the name of diversity, multiculturalism, equality, social justice, and so on, amounts to nothing more than a naked reach for power by special interest groups that have not earned the right to be dominant. The supporters of the social justice movement—the "social justice warriors" (SJWs)—are not interested in the betterment of mankind. Their objective is social control. The minority peoples who perceive themselves as victims want to be the victors. Those at the bottom want to be at the top. Those who identify as "oppressed" want to trade places with their oppressors.

It is a twist on the Spartacus story, in which Roman slaves sought relief from Roman oppression by fighting for their freedom. Identity politics is where Spartacus and his followers want to become the masters by transforming their masters into slaves. Welcome to the tyranny of the minority.

It should be understood that the Left, thanks to its quasi-religious nature, does not exhibit tolerance for different viewpoints or lifestyles. Everyone is expected to share similar beliefs. If you don't, you are subject to censorship and harassment. Compromise is nonexistent. The goal of the Left is elimination of non-leftist viewpoints. The dominant whites are not to be eliminated as long as they run around confessing their white privilege and accepting white guilt.

Traditional morality of the American variety celebrates taking personal responsibility as opposed to blaming others. Being a victim occupies a negative place in the hierarchy of values. But the new progressive morality of the Left—what I call the victim mentality, what others have called the "victimhood culture"—celebrates victimhood. "If you are a victim," says Scott Greer, "you are now a hero thanks to our society's transvaluation of values."

Greer compares social justice warriors with the Puritans who settled Massachusetts. They are dogmatic, self-righteous, intolerant of different views, and demanding of conformity. "They love witch hunts," Greer says. "They even have their own form of original sin: being born white, which requires constant atonement." Tammy Bruce, in *The New Thought Police*, agrees that social justice has become a method for protecting special groups against the perceived injustice allegedly perpetrated by heterosexual, white males.

Thomas Sowell has a penetrating observation in *Wealth, Poverty and Politics* that groups in all cultures exhibit resentment against those in a superior position, who must be brought down. Usually, Sowell says, it takes the form of a majority that resents a successful minority, as with the Germans and the Jews, or the Ottomans and the Armenians. But in our case, the minorities that lag behind are conducting the witch hunt against the successful white majority.

Tolerance vs. Celebration

Social justice warriors have confused tolerance with acquiescence and celebration. Tolerance for a minority group should not imply that the majority must accept and celebrate minority viewpoints. I can be tolerant of gays, for example, without praising their lifestyle or agreeing that we should change the accepted definition of marriage to suit the LGBTQ political agenda. I can be tolerant of African-Americans without celebrating "black power" or listening to rap music.

We are being deceived because minority mouthpieces are not satisfied with tolerance or equality. They want celebration and subservience. They want to impose their minority agendas on the rest of us. Gloria Steinem won't be satisfied with equal pay for women; she believes that "the best man for the job is a woman." Rev. Al Sharpton is not interested in equality under the law for African-Americans; he wants to run the show, to be "more equal." Muslims don't want to fit into American culture; they want to supplant the Constitution with sharia. Gays are not satisfied with mainstream acceptance; they want to dictate to the society how to define marriage. What better way to accomplish these goals than by siding with the Left to convince the rest of us that our traditional values are for the birds.

The Crazy People Are Taking Over the Asylum

Take, for example, the politically liberal City of Northampton, Massachusetts, where they recently launched an excellent program to improve community-police relations. For several months, police officers were dispatched to the local elementary school every Friday where they greeted the kids with a "high five." A *Fox News* video showed the children getting a kick out of interacting with the jovial cops. It was nice for the entire community. But not for long.

After *one parent* objected, the city authorities became concerned that the popular "High Five Friday" program might "intimidate" some children. The Northampton Police Department issued the following statement: "Concerns were shared that some kids might respond negatively to a group of uniformed officers at their school. People were specifically concerned about kids of color, undocumented children, or any children who may have had negative experiences with the police."

So they cancelled the whole thing.

What is really noteworthy about this incident is that Northampton was not inundated with protests or tons of criticism. "High Five Friday" was a big hit with the community. The vast majority loved it. According to *Fox News*, only one parent complained. This is the insidious nature of political correctness. The minority interests in this case succeeded in imposing self-censorship on the majority without lifting a finger. The police state mentality existed in the minds of the city administrators. Believing that their high five program was politically incorrect, the powers-that-be enforced the will of the minority without the need for outside intervention. George Orwell's prediction of "thought crime" was realized.

Bill O'Reilly, on Fox's *O'Reilly Factor*, was outraged by the Northampton affair. "When did the country allow the crazy people to take over?" he asked. "The crazy people are now running this country. We've lost control." The crazy people seem to be successful in pushing their agenda at our institutions of higher learning. American colleges and universities are hot beds of political correctness where liberal ideas are accepted and conservative ones are ostracized. Attorney Alan Dershowitz has referred to this as a "curtain of McCarthyism" that is descending over college campuses.

A disgraceful example of the tyranny of the minority occurred at UCLA. A well-regarded professor was disciplined for insisting that his students use the *Chicago Manual of Style*, which is de rigueur for English composition. A sit-in by a group of black students claimed it was offensive and racist. In a shameful reaction, the school's administration supported the ridiculous claims of the "offended" students. "UCLA's response to the sit-ins was a travesty of justice," wrote author Heather Mac Donald in *City Journal*. "Asking for better grammar is inflammatory in the school," said an intimidated UCLA teaching assistant. "You have to give an A or you're a racist."

At the University of Missouri, a group of minority students created a furor when they demanded a faculty that is a minimum of 10% black. They also demanded the addition of a mandatory "awareness and inclusion" curriculum developed by nonwhite students and faculty. "They want to dictate the academic offerings of a university," said Julius Kairey of the *Heritage Foundation*, "with special treatment for their own racial groups." That is more evidence that the radical Left wants power, Kairey concluded, not equality.

A group of black students occupied a building at UC Santa Cruz, an illegal act. In addition to separate dormitories for black students, they demanded that all students go through a mandatory in-person "diversity competency training" that would be reviewed and approved by the black students. "We demand that every incoming student complete this training by their first day of class." Instead of arresting the protestors, the cowardly administration agreed to all the demands. The black students effectively assumed control of the campus. Indoctrinating students in the Left's agenda of diversity—which really amounts to marginalizing white people—is totalitarian and racist.

To advance their objectives, minority special interests invented white privilege and toxic masculinity. As in the Northampton case, many white men and women—who ought to be offended—have internalized these concepts and will defend them against people like me, who view them as toxic examples of identity politics. Yes, many gullible whites have fallen for this liberal deception. They are ashamed to be white and apologize every chance they get. One white woman has received a lot of media coverage because she insists that she is black. Although her white parents dispute this nonsense, she sports an afro, wears lots of dark makeup, and served as president of the local NAACP chapter. Welcome to our brave new world.

White is a Color Too

The crazy people may not be so crazy after all. They want power and they are getting it. White people, especially males, are being demonized and marginalized by liberals and the PC gang (one and the same). As a defense against this form of racism, I have become an advocate for white people. Thirty years ago, I would have been scandalized even to contemplate embracing such a concept. Things have changed. Now when I defend white Americans, I am advocating the excellent value system established by white people in the US. I am not referring to white supremacism. That would be the Ku Klux Klan—no thank you. I'm referring to the achievements of white people, especially white men, throughout our history.

White men founded our republic. White men ended slavery in this country. White men are largely responsible for the day-to-day commerce that puts food on the table and clothing on our backs. America runs because of white people and their value system. Like it or not, white people drive the engine that makes this country work.

In contrast, look at teenagers in the black subculture who abhor the very idea of adopting white values. The worst insult for these kids is to be called "Whitey" or "Uncle Tom." This self-destructive behavior is ruining the lives of millions of black kids. It is reinforced by political correctness, which bashes white men every chance it gets.

More and more people have figured out that the old excuses for black crime and mayhem—jobs, poverty, schooling, etc.—are not working anymore. "Now they have a new excuse," says Colin Flaherty in *Don't Make the Black Kids Angry*. "The ultimate excuse: White racism is everywhere. White racism is permanent. White racism explains everything." White America has been mostly passive about this blitz of anti-white allegations—perhaps because of white guilt, perhaps because of fear of violent reprisals. It is time to declare that white people are victimized by racism and ought to be designated as a special class. And by the way— someone should explain to people of color that white is a color too.

Incidentally, what is your definition of racist? This term is largely misunderstood. Here are two definitions of racism:

1. The classical definition of racism: denigrating a group of people without credible evidence.
2. The PC definition of racism: *any criticism* of a protected class of people. Evidence in support of the criticism doesn't make it acceptable.

According to the PC definition, I am a racist because I have the effrontery to criticize the behavior of minorities. The R word no longer holds the kind of opprobrium that it did in the 1960s. It has been tossed around so carelessly that it no longer packs a punch. "Yesterday's race-baiters were brutal white bullies," says Ben Shapiro. "Today's are left-wingers invoking fictional white racism to achieve their goals." I'm actually rather proud to be considered a racist by the PC gang because it means that I am still using my brain.

Women and the Left

Barack Obama masked his socialist, anti-American agenda with the devious "Hope and Change" mantra. He was able to seduce millions of "liberal" voters. After eight years, the electorate finally awakened from the nightmare. Obama's agenda—the Left's agenda—was voted down in the 2016 presidential election. No matter. The Left wants to perpetuate its values by whatever means are necessary. For the Left, the end justifies the means. They don't care what we—the people who voted for Trump—think. Remember, the Left is against individual rights and the rule of law. The Left is totalitarian. They want to revert to the socialist model and to hell with what the voters have to say about it.

DIVERSITY: DIVIDE AND CONQUER

Enter the "Women's March." Women from across the nation descended on Washington, DC, to protest their "victimhood." The Left has frightened these decent women, telling them that their rights are being taken away by the Republicans. Of course, no one is quite sure exactly what rights are being withheld. It doesn't matter. Once they accepted this emotional argument, the marchers fell into line and were swept away by the leftist agenda. The Women's March is a tribute to the gullibility of large segments of our population. Ostensibly the women were marching for women's rights, but in reality the march was organized by a cadre of leftist special interests with the aim of imposing their agenda on the majority. Look at the predominance of the disaffected among the list of speakers: Angela Davis, Van Jones, Gloria Steinem, Michael Moore. Listen to the angry, vicious hate speech...all in the name of "love." This is a good example of how the Left often manipulates the unwary majority into agreeing with them.

What do these leftists want? Michael Moore revealed the truth when he said that "what we need" in government are women (i.e., liberal women), blacks, Hispanics, gays, transgenders, etc. Falsely posing as a movement of inclusion, the Women's March is actually a movement of exclusion. Men, heterosexuals, and conservative women are distinctly not wanted. I can hear Elizabeth Warren screaming, "We've had it with guys like you!" The Left does not want alpha males like Donald Trump. They want feminized men like Michael Moore. And what kind of women do they want? Elizabeth Warren, Hillary Clinton, Nancy Pelosi, Maxine Waters, Kamala Harris.

President Trump is portrayed as misogynistic, racist, anti-Semitic. Rachel Maddow on MSNBC compared Trump to Adolf Hitler. The majority of voters don't buy all this nonsense, but the *New York Times* does. The next Women's

March should be supported by a full-page ad in the *Times* that says, "The best man for the job is a woman." Let's face it, the march's organizers are angry that a woman was not elected president.

The anti-Trump hysteria has been cooked up by the Left, supported by the left-leaning mainstream media, and swallowed whole by decent women who seem to be living in denial of reality. Frankly, I am sympathetic to the feminist pro-choice position, but today's reality is that abortion is no longer the main issue facing the country. Immigration, crime, and Islamic terrorism are the big issues. The Women's March accuses Trump of discrimination against Mexicans and Muslims because he wants to protect our borders. He is accused of anti-black racism because he believes in the rule of law. The organizers of the march would like to see millions of illegal aliens pouring across the Rio Grande accompanied by riots and looting in the black communities.

And so now we come to the real hypocrisy of the Women's March. By taking the position that Trump is a racist, their intention is to further divide a country that is already suffering from the divisive policies of the Obama administration. By taking a position against "Islamophobia," they are granting their approval to the planet's number one abuser of women, Islam. If these women want to protest policies and behaviors that disregard women's rights, why don't they go after the treatment of women under the banner of the Islamic religion? As Kay Hymowitz wrote in *City Journal*: "Where are the demonstrations, the articles, the petitions, the resolutions, the vindications of the rights of Islamic women by American feminists?"

There is an obvious reason for this hypocrisy. If they would speak out against the treatment of women under Islam, feminists would be obliged to acknowledge the progress that has been made for women's rights in the West.

That would detract from their coveted victim status. By keeping quiet, feminists are colluding with Muslims who want to bring sharia—with its degrading policies toward women—to our shores. Here lies the sad irony inherent in the Women's March. Instead of improving the condition of women, the Leftist agenda ultimately would destroy all the gains made by women in the past half century.

From Superpower to Sitting Duck

In an assault on homeland security, the progressive religion strives to perpetuate Obama's attempt to bring America down. Obama's self-identification as a globalist gave him the right—in his eyes—to put America's interests behind everybody else's. Globalism, as Mark Levin points out, is all about surrendering aspects of our sovereignty. Decisions would be made by international bureaucrats who do not have the needs of America in mind. Instead of being free to act in its own interests, the US "should relinquish its hard-earned position in favor of multilateral power sharing," says Levin in *Liberty and Tyranny*. "In this way, America's interests are subsumed and contained by the supposed interests of the whole."

The leftist concept of going borderless denies the benefits of being a nation state, especially for those nation states that consider themselves to be democracies. All we have to do is look at the European Union to see how the tyranny of unelected bureaucrats can destroy the sovereignty of individual nations. The administrative edicts of the EU take precedence over laws passed by the duly elected representatives of member states. The implications for the citizens of France or Germany or Holland are alarming. Those citizens are no longer living in a democracy. Brussels is calling the shots. "Constitutional government—to say nothing of liberal democracy," says Professor Edward J. Erler, "will not be a part of the politically correct, borderless world into which so many of our political leaders wish to usher us."

Trump, unlike Obama, is defending our sovereignty by making America first. He has declared that he is president of the US, not president of the world. This is a critical distinction for anyone who believes in the American Constitution and the rights of the individual.

Lying again to the American people, Obama declared that we have nothing to fear from Islamic terrorism. As former CIA officer and political strategist Clare Lopez pointed out, Obama's policies with respect to the Islamic world favored our enemies and undermined our allies. His policy for the defense establishment exposed his desire to level the playing field. The US Army was cut back to the smallest force since before the World War II buildup. Thanks to Obama, the US Navy has fewer ships than it had when we entered World War I in 1917.

Slashing our military budget makes us more vulnerable and encourages aggression by our enemies. Cutting back American power plays into the hands of Islamic terrorists and others who wish us ill. But it fits in beautifully with the Left's agenda. The liberal playbook, if allowed to grow in power and influence, will undermine the value system that has sustained the US for more than 200 years.

Chapter Four
Free Speech vs. Political Correctness

In the first chapter, I expressed my view that freedom of speech is the keystone of all our rights and privileges. We are fortunate to have the First Amendment to the Constitution:

> "Congress shall make no law respecting an establishment of religion, or prohibiting the free exercise thereof; or abridging the freedom of speech, or of the press; or the right of the people peaceably to assemble, and to petition the Government for a redress of grievances."

The courts and the legislature have been protective of free speech and reluctant to dilute First Amendment protection except for limited applications. One of them is known as the Smith Act (1940), which made it illegal to advocate the overthrow of the government by force and violence. A distinction was made between advocacy of ideas and advocacy of action. Speech was protected in the former but not in the latter. You can make a speech about overthrowing the government as long as you don't drive the audience to violent action. Oh, and you can't yell FIRE in a crowded theater. Aside from that, you can say pretty much anything you like.

As of this writing, free speech is under attack everywhere in the world. The US is not immune to this disease. For years, I have been warning about the Democratic Party's campaign to destroy the First Amendment. This is not a new development. When Democratic President Woodrow Wilson brought the US into World War I, he tried to censor anti-war sentiments by ushering the Sedition Act through Congress. It outlawed any "disloyal or abusive language" about the US government or the military. Strange as it may seem today, says Ben Shapiro, tens of thousands were arrested by the Justice Department under the Sedition Act.

The Democrats under Obama tried to silence anyone who opposed important liberal positions. You could get yourself in hot water if you denied global warming, criticized Islamic terrorism, or advocated a stronger military. The Democratic-controlled California legislature has come dangerously close to passing a law that would authorize prosecutors to sue fossil fuel companies, think tanks, and individuals who have "deceived or misled the public on the risks of climate change."

That means I could wind up in jail for writing my book, *In Lies We Trust*, wherein I argue that global warming is a giant hoax. Me? Go to jail simply for expressing my opinion? It must be a joke. Never mind that I offer an overwhelming raft of evidence in support of my position, never mind that global warming is anything but "incontrovertible" (as the leaders of the Democratic Party would suggest), never mind the First Amendment—I could be put behind bars because of my contrarian viewpoint and *for no other reason*. In other words, *freedom of speech is one step away from annihilation*.

Here is another example: On the heels of the San Bernardino killings, citing a "wonderful opportunity and wonderful moment to really make *significant change*" (my italics), Obama's Attorney General Loretta Lynch expressed her concern about what she called the "incredibly disturbing rise of anti-Muslim rhetoric... that fear is my greatest fear." She was not worried about terrorism. Her *greatest fear* was that we might experience an Islamophobic backlash. In a warning to those who engage in unapproved speech, Lynch said that she would take "aggressive action" against anyone whose speech she interpreted as "anti-Muslim rhetoric." "Unfortunately," wrote David French in the *National Review*, "when the Constitution conflicts with the demands of social justice, discarding the Bill of Rights is part of the Obama administration's mission statement."

Can you comprehend the overwhelming importance of this issue? The choice is either democracy or something else entirely. (Let me give you a hint. It is called *totalitarianism*.) If the government succeeds in making it unlawful today to take a skeptical position on climate change or to criticize Islam, it can be unlawful tomorrow to express a contrary view on *any topic that the government wants to control*.

Once freedom of speech goes, that is the end. We may never get it back. Without freedom of speech, we have no rights, no liberties, no freedoms. Orwell's prediction in *Nineteen Eighty-Four* will have been realized—Big Brother will tell us what to think. Is that what we want for our country?

You think I am exaggerating? Just look at how Obama used censorship to advance his political ideology. Refusing to acknowledge that deadly terrorist attacks are Islamic in origin, Obama ordered all federal agencies and departments to cease using these words and phrases: *Islamic, radical Islamic terrorism, jihad, sharia, Allah*. In his book, *See Something Say Nothing*, former Department of Homeland Security officer Philip Haney suggests that the San Bernardino attack might have been prevented if Obama had not crippled DHS's intelligence gathering with his politically correct censorship. How can we fight an enemy when we are not allowed to discuss who and what the enemy is? It is simply impossible. The sooner we acknowledge the problem, the sooner we will be able to solve it.

Deliberate attempts by the Obama administration to limit free speech pale in comparison to the rise of *political correctness*. Political correctness is an underhanded technique of the Left whose purpose is to shut down any speech that is not in accord with the liberal playbook. PC is purely totalitarian and will, if permitted to flourish, destroy the Constitution and put us in the same cesspool as Venezuela. The term political correctness is said to have been coined by Chinese dictator Mao Zedong. Those who deviated from the Chinese Communist Party line, who expressed views that were politically incorrect, were subjected to harsh disciplinary measures. Now it's our turn to suffer.

Before I offer a definition of PC, here is an example: During the 2016 election campaign, Sen. Elizabeth Warren served as Hillary Clinton's attack dog. Did you hear Warren's sexist, foul-mouthed, hypocritical attack on Donald Trump? She chastised him for calling Hillary a "nasty woman." Former Education Secretary Bill Bennett put Trump's comment in perspective when he said, "Hillary Clinton is a woman and she is nasty, so what's the problem?" Warren didn't quite see it that way.

Sounding like she was infected by a rabid dog, Warren screamed at Trump, "We've had it with guys like you!" *Guys like you.* Can you imagine? Warren was parroting Hillary's boast that she has "a lot of experience dealing with men who sometimes get off the reservation." Imagine if Trump had said: "We've had it with dames who don't know their place." Or: "Broads like you." That would have been politically incorrect. The Dems and their media enablers would have had a hernia.

It is entirely acceptable to call a man "nasty" or any other derogatory term, but when applied to a woman, it is forbidden. This double standard is an example of political correctness in action. Who the hell are Warren or Clinton to tell us what words we can use or where we can or can't use those words? Sexist statements such as "guys like you" had the approval of Hillary's leftist supporters who pushed the mindless argument that we need a woman as president, even if that woman is an unindicted felon. Another double standard. If I had argued that we need a man as president, the Hillary gang would have locked me in the Bastille and thrown away the key.

Political Correctness Defined

Here is the definition of political correctness: an unofficial code of conduct that supports progressive ideals by avoiding language and behavior that are perceived as offensive, discriminatory, or judgmental with regard to specially designated groups of people. As the Elizabeth Warren example shows, women are one of the designated groups and men are not. The racial component of PC is that minorities generally are exempt. PC empowers specially designated classes while enslaving those who don't fall into a special category, especially white males.

As I said, PC is inherently tyrannical. For many on the Left, "the power structures of a racist-sexist-ableist-queerphobic etc. society are so oppressive," wrote Andrew Sullivan in *New York Magazine*, "that non-p.c. speech is the equivalent of violence, and so must be shut down."

PC has a close cousin in *microaggression*, used by minority groups as a silencing tactic against free speech. Microaggression describes insults, intentional or unintentional, by whites against blacks, women, gays, or any other socially marginalized or protected group. Examples include: "America is the land of opportunity" and "I believe the most qualified person should get the job." It's hard to believe that these statements are considered offensive, but they are. It shows how crazy the whole business has become.

The concept of microaggression implies that dominance is deviant behavior, says *Daily Caller* editor Scott Greer. Victimhood is virtuous; dominance and privilege are deviant. The offending conduct allegedly perpetuates the domination of special groups by the privileged white culture.

Offensive statements do not have to be overt, as in use of the N word. It can be something as innocuous as "good morning." What counts is the subjective reaction of the offended person. Presumption of guilt means that the alleged offender is not given an opportunity to defend himself. "This is a secular theory of original sin," says British sociologist Frank Furedi, "from which no white, heterosexual man can possibly escape." If you ignore or question someone's claim of having been offended, you are guilty of "victim-blaming." It is a no-win situation for white people.

Here is another example of PC: Tucker Carlson, on his Fox show, reported a PC attack against free speech in Montgomery County, Maryland. The ruckus centered on the rape of a child by an illegal alien. Instead of deploring the crime, Superintendent of Schools Jack R. Smith sent out an email reflecting what Carlson calls the "same old diversity agenda"—that hate speech against illegals would be punished severely. Students were encouraged to report any cases of "offensive messages" to the proper authorities. "Hate-based incidents are on the rise across this country," Smith said as he urged students to participate in a contest denouncing "hate," a term that apparently encompasses any political expression that school administrators disagree with.

Never mind going after rapists or other people who break the law. Just go after freedom of speech.

Do you remember when facts were facts? To the PC mindset, facts are interpreted as having political ramifications. If you say that the sun is shining, the PC gang will interpret your statement relative to social or economic conditions. Rep. Maxine Waters might argue, for example, that the sun may be shining for some people but not for others who are less fortunate. Thanks to political correctness, truth is relative and reality is negotiable. The Left wants you to accept its version of reality.

Political correctness is the heir to McCarthyism, an attempt by the Right to shut down the Left during the 1950s "red scare." The target of McCarthyism was anyone who was suspected of being a communist or communist sympathizer. Ironically, political correctness is an attempt by the Left to shut down the Right. The wheel has turned.

Here are some more examples of political correctness:

- According to the Equal Employment Opportunity Commission, it is illegal for employers to discriminate against criminals because it has a "disproportionate" impact on minorities.
- A California high school sent five students home for wearing shirts that displayed the American flag on the Mexican holiday of Cinco de Mayo.
- A high school track team was disqualified because one of the runners "made a gesture thanking God" once he had crossed the finish line.
- More than 75% of the babies born in Detroit are born to unmarried women, yet it is considered to be politically incorrect to suggest that there is anything wrong with that.
- An Arizona student's paper received a lower grade because she used the word, "mankind," instead of a gender-

neutral term for humanity.
- A UK council banned the term "brainstorming" and replaced it with "thought showers" because local lawmakers thought the term might offend epileptics.
- A UK job advertisement for "reliable" and "hard-working" applicants was rejected by the job center as it could be offensive to unreliable and lazy people.
- Santa Clauses in Sydney, Australia, were banned from saying "Ho, ho, ho" because it could be offensive to women who noticed the similarity to the American slang for prostitute.

In Orwell's novel, *Nineteen Eighty-Four*, the language of the totalitarian state is called *Newspeak*, and it bears a striking resemblance to political correctness. The objective of Newspeak was to control thoughts and opinions. It was enforced in Orwell's fictional world by the *Thought Police*. The difference today is that the Thought Police are unnecessary because political correctness is used by the Left to enforce self-censorship. The police state is in your own mind. If you believe that your thoughts are politically incorrect, you will banish them without the need for outside intervention. Orwell's prediction of *thought crime* has been realized.

Now for the really scary news: *Pew Research Center* reports that 40% of millennials are in favor of government-enforced prohibition not merely of offensive speech, but also viewpoints that may offend minorities. Twenty years ago, I would have asked, how do you prohibit a viewpoint? Today it is all too clear—thanks to PC.

Political correctness is completely in tune with the modus operandi of the Left, which has no use for free speech or the truth. All the Left cares about is the advancement of its objectives. When you contradict them, leftists will immediately fire back with a pejorative label. "Look around you," said Tammy Bruce in *The New Thought Police*. "Labels such as racist, sexist, and homophobe are routinely used to demonize anyone who utters a word that doesn't support the Left's agenda."

As Mark Steyn has pointed out, the classic Left response is, "Let's not debate your point of view, let's cancel your point of view." The constitutional absolute right to free expression, Steyn says, "is of limited value in a litigious society where people can tie you up in court from 5 to 10 years. There's no point in having absolute freedom of speech if as a practical matter public discourse shrivels to an ever narrower range of opinion."

So be careful what you say because someone on the Left may be listening. This is what the American people were going to get if they put Hillary Clinton in the Oval Office. If Hillary had succeeded in censoring what we can and can't say on certain issues, she would have enjoyed a clear path to outlawing ANY opinions that contradict those of the Left. Recent laws passed in Congress authorize the detention and torture of American citizens who are suspected of having ties to terrorist organizations. These laws could easily be expanded to include anyone who calls Hillary "nasty."

Clinton and Warren are not the only Democrats who have no use for free speech. Sen. Bernie Sanders is not far behind. "Criminalizing things is very much on Bernie's agenda, beginning with the criminalization of political dissent," says *National Review*. "At every event he swears to introduce a constitutional amendment reversing Supreme Court decisions that affirmed the free-speech protections of people and organizations. That this would amount to a repeal of the First Amendment does not trouble Bernie at all."

Drink Your Coca-Cola and Keep Your Mouth Shut

Along with Coca-Cola, McDonald's, and Disneyland, political correctness has become a popular American export. "If you talk about immigration," said one French politician, "you're a xenophobe. If you talk about security, you're a fascist. If you talk about Islam, you're an Islamophobe." Too bad we can't put a dollar value on PC—we could turn around the US trade deficit overnight.

We should observe what is happening in Europe because it raises the alarm bell for what might happen here. Many European countries already have laws on the books that proscribe certain forms of speech. Traditionally liberal Holland has effectively instituted state censorship. Parliamentary leader Geert Wilders was convicted of hate speech for suggesting that Muslim immigration should be terminated. Opponents of a Dutch plan to establish asylum centers for Middle Eastern refugees have received police visits at home. Imagine the police knocking on your door to threaten that you could be arrested for your opinions. A German couple was convicted and sentenced for creating a Facebook page that criticized the government's immigration policy. Swedes are afraid to speak openly about immigrant-related crimes because of a so-called anti-hate law in that country. Actress Brigitte Bardot has been convicted and fined five times for violating a French law that prohibits criticism of Islam. An English election candidate was arrested on suspicion of "racial harassment" when he quoted a critical passage about Islam. The source of the quote: Winston Churchill.

"In Europe, is the enemy now the governments?" asks *Gatestone Institute*. "Evidence is mounting that expressing even a mild opinion that runs counter to official government policy can land you in prison, or at least ensure a visit from your friendly local Kafkaesque police. Has Europe effectively become a police state?"

The situation in Holland has become a cause celebre thanks to Geert Wilders. Wilders, who leads the right-wing Dutch Party for Freedom, has been a vocal critic of Islam and Muslim immigration. His outspoken disdain for the changing demographics in the Netherlands has resulted in numerous death threats. Wilders now lives like a prisoner in his own country. Every day, he and his wife are ferried around to secret locations in military bases and safe houses by a special detachment of the Dutch police.

As though Wilders' disrupted lifestyle were not a sufficient price to pay for speaking his mind, a Dutch court in 2011 attempted to convict him of hate speech when he compared Islam with fascism. The Netherlands is cursed with liberal "hate speech" laws that prohibit criticism of religion. Happily, the case against Wilders was eventually thrown out. I remember being relieved at the time. My fear was that freedom of speech was dead in, of all places, tolerant little Holland. I was right to be afraid. The Dutch judicial system went after him once more in 2016 when Wilders asked a crowd in The Hague if they wanted fewer Moroccans in the Netherlands. And this time they got him. A Dutch court convicted Wilders of "insulting a group and inciting discrimination." Although the court did not impose a punishment, the precedent was set for placing limitations on free speech.

"The Netherlands has become a sick country," said Wilders in reaction to the court that convicted him. "You have restricted the freedom of speech for millions of Dutch. But fortunately, truth and liberty are stronger than you." He may be wrong about that. The assault on individual rights is supported by the European Union with convictions under similar hate laws occurring in France and the UK. What these restrictive court decisions are actually doing is masking a reluctance on the part of European countries to acknowledge the threat posed by Muslim immigration. The open border policy in the Netherlands, for example, has spawned dozens of crime-ridden "no-go" zones throughout Holland because so many of the Muslim immigrants refuse to assimilate. In her book, *Infidel*, former Muslim Ayaan Hirsi Ali describes the plight of thousands of women and children in Holland who are being "systematically abused," beaten half to death, or even killed by their Muslim husbands, fathers, and boyfriends while the state looks the other way. Holland hides behind its anti-hate laws to avoid taking responsibility for the calamity that is taking place within its borders. Anyone who mentions the problem of Muslim immigration is automatically accused of racism.

The winner in all this, believe it or not, is Islam. When freedom of speech is curtailed because Muslims complain they are being victimized, it plays into what is known as "civilizational jihad"—the attempt to transform Western societies so they can be brought under the control of Islamic law, known as sharia. Sharia does not recognize freedom of speech, nor does it accept any concept of individual rights as embraced by the West. The self-destructive policies of European countries, led by Angela Merkel's open door policy in Germany, are collaborating with the Muslim hardliners who seek to destroy Western Civilization. (see Chapter Eight)

As in the United States, the European left is attacking free speech and the right is defending. One unintended result of Geert Wilders' conviction is that it may backfire by fueling support for right-wing parties throughout Europe. Wilders' Party for Freedom just won 20 seats in Parliament. He could be Holland's prime minister in the next election.

Enough is Too Much

The Left is aware that PC has been exposed as a tool for shutting down free expression. Here is their defense of PC (from a left-wing blog):

> "Through portraying PC as something forced down the throats of societies, anti-PC politicians not only discredit an expression but also undermine the idea behind it. In principle, political correctness intends to contribute to greater social equality and fairness. Yet this notion of PC has become obscure in contemporary political discussions. In this situation, it is harder than ever for the idea of PC to win hearts and minds."

My response to this quote: Yes, PC is being forced down our throats; and, yes, it must be undermined for the sake of free speech; and no, PC does not contribute to social equality and fairness—it attempts to endow the minority with censorship over majority opinions.

British commentator Pat Condell thinks PC has already gone too far. "We've had enough of political correctness, of being told what we're supposed to think and say," insists Condell. "We've had enough of being made to feel there's something wrong with us for wanting to preserve our way of life. We want honesty, we want the truth, and we'll take it where we can find it."

Author BJ Gallagher, writing in the liberal *Huffington Post*, says that although the original intent of political correctness may have been to encourage tact and sensitivity to others' feelings, the effect has been to hinder our ability to live with those who are different from us. "It's gone so far that political correctness has become a bigger problem than the problem it was intended to address," Gallagher argues.

"Consider the impact of your censorship and finger-wagging, as well as your inclination to self-righteous, moral indignation. You don't realize it, but you're essentially imposing a gag order on the whole of American society."

Chapter Five
It's Not My Fault:
Avoiding Personal Responsibility

Recently I ate breakfast at the "locals" place I've been going to for more than 20 years. In a bit right out of the Jack Nicholson movie, *As Good As It Gets*, my waitress for most of that time has been Susan, who could pass for a screwball comedienne like Judy Holliday. On this particular day, Susan was not being funny. As usual, I ordered my eggs scrambled soft with pork sausage patties and an English muffin. After an interminable wait, Susan came out of the kitchen with my soft scrambled eggs and chicken sausage links.

"Hey Susan," I said, "This isn't what I ordered. I ordered sausage patties."

Instead of apologizing, Susan made a face and barked at me with, "I wish you would say you don't want chicken sausages!" She grabbed the plate and returned a few minutes later with hot sausage patties, cold eggs, and a petrified English muffin, which she unceremoniously slammed down on the table.

Susan's unspoken message was: "It wasn't my fault for getting the order incorrectly, it was your fault because you didn't specify what you *didn't* want." Of course, I didn't want bacon, nor did I want ham, steak, or pork chops. Was I supposed to list all of them?

Susan was acting out what seems to be a social problem of epidemic proportions: Don't take responsibility for your behavior. Don't apologize for screwing up, just blame it on somebody else. It's much simpler and in the short term it can do wonders for your self-esteem. Right, Susan?

This attitude of blaming is what I call the *victim mentality*: the unwillingness to take responsibility for one's own behavior and instead blaming others for life's problems. This argument defies logic and the facts. Being a victim is a choice, not an inevitability. No one is a victim unless he chooses to be. What distinguishes humans from "animals" is the ability to choose, to make decisions. When faced with an obstacle, we are challenged with the decision either to (a) overcome the obstacle, or (b) become a victim. When you choose to overcome the obstacle, you are accepting personal responsibility for your life. If you choose to be a victim, your choice implies that someone else has control over your life. "It's not my fault, it's the fault of..." When you choose to be a victim, you deny that you have the power to change your life for the better... so you give up.

Taking personal responsibility has always been one of the key American values. Remember the myth of the rugged individual? "Americans viewed themselves as masters of their own fate," political economist Nicholas Eberstadt wrote in *Foreign Affairs*, "intensely proud because they were self-reliant." Today you have to look pretty hard to find rugged individuals. In their place we have a culture of dependency. Thanks in large measure to the leftist policies of Democratic administrations, the habit of assuming responsibility has gradually been fading away. More and more, we are sending the message to new generations that it is acceptable to avoid taking responsibility. You don't even have to be responsible for your own survival. Your parents will support you or the government will give you free stuff or you will win the lottery.

Susan's eagerness to blame me for her mistake is symptomatic of the problem. Unless we decide to advocate in favor of accepting personal responsibility, our civilization will implode and I will never get my breakfast served properly.

What Happened to that Damned Cherry Tree?

One of the foundational myths of the USA is the apocryphal story of how George Washington chopped down the cherry tree. When his father confronted him, Washington confessed. "I cannot tell a lie, Father," he said. "I cut down your cherry tree." It is an allegory with two messages: the virtue of truthfulness, and the virtue of taking responsibility for one's actions rather than blaming someone else. The myth of the rugged individual comes out of this story. Americans have always prided themselves on being self-reliant. They used to regard poverty as "a temporary challenge that could be overcome with determination and character," said Nicholas Eberstadt, "with enterprise, hard work, and grit." Ironically, it was a Democratic president—Harry Truman—who said, "The buck stops here."

"The idea that people who simply choose not to work should be supported by money taken from those who are working was rejected across the ideological spectrum," said economist Thomas Sowell. That's how it used to be. Over the past several generations, according to Nicholas Eberstadt, "the remarkable growth of the entitlement state has radically transformed both the American government and the American way of life itself."

The Left wants to reinvent the cherry tree story. In the

leftist version, Washington blames his friend, an African-American boy who is a slave on the family plantation, for cutting down the tree. His friend is punished severely while George gets off scot-free by virtue of his white privilege. Instead of leading the Continental Army to victory in the Revolutionary War, Washington moves to Chicago, becomes a community organizer, and goes on welfare for the next 30 years.

One of the disturbing signs of our times, says Thomas Sowell, is the raft of government programs "that relieve people of the necessity of working to provide their own livelihoods." Today's welfare state got its start with the expansion of government programs under FDR's New Deal. LBJ's Great Society and War on Poverty expanded many of these programs in the 1960s. Obama made sure that Americans got the point with his famous quip, "If you've got a business—you didn't build that. Somebody else made that happen." An unfortunate lesson implied by Obama's statement is, "If I can't take credit for my accomplishments, then I don't have to take responsibility for my failures."

Relieving people of personal responsibility for their own lives is part of the Left's plan to make us all dependent on big government. The belief that "people are *entitled* to what others have produced," says Thomas Sowell, "is at the heart of the social degeneration that can be traced back to the 1960s. Teenage pregnancies, venereal diseases, dependency on government and murder rates were all going down during the much disdained 1950s. All reversed and shot up as the welfare state, and the social vision behind the welfare state, took over in the 1960s."

The bad news is that the Left has already accomplished most of its objective. "We've gotten to the point," said the man who called television a *vast wasteland*, Newton Minow, "where everybody's got a right and nobody's got a responsibility." Susan's unwillingness to take responsibility for screwing up my breakfast order is but a tiny reflection of how American ethics have changed. More and more Americans are embracing the victim mentality. Obama blamed most of his failures on Bush. Hillary blamed her election loss on James Comey, the Russians, and Wikileaks. A young woman has sued her law school because she was unable to get a job after graduation. African-American leaders like Al Sharpton argue that blacks are over-represented in the prison population not because of the high black crime rate but because of white privilege and white racism.

Referring to the lack of responsibility by African-American men, the *Heritage Foundation* has identified "the largest-scale abandonment of women by men in human history, what's happening all through this country." Half of the pregnancies in Washington, DC, end in abortion. Of those who are born, 70 percent are born outside of wedlock. The black family, claims the *Heritage Foundation*, was destroyed by "the progressive term 'compassion' during the 'War on Poverty,' which began in 1964."

According to *Forbes*, the American welfare state looks like "a vast empire bigger than the entire budgets of almost every other country in the world." The *Census Bureau* estimates our current welfare spending equals four times the cash required to eliminate all poverty in America. However, says *Forbes*, the poverty rate is "substantially higher than when the War on Poverty began. In other words, we fought the War on Poverty, and poverty won."

The number of African-American lives damaged or destroyed by Democratic welfare policies, says David Horowitz, "would exceed the wildest dreams of any Klansman." The legacy of the Left's welfare system is:

- break-up of low-income families
- explosion of out-of-wedlock births
- systemic poverty
- higher crime and rates of incarceration
- substantial decrease in the number of low-income households headed by someone who works

As a result of Obama's plan to redistribute income, 96% of Americans now benefit from some kind of social program. The premise of redistribution, according to Charles Murray in *Coming Apart*, is that successful people don't deserve what they have achieved—"they got it because they were born into the right social stratum. Thus it is morally appropriate to require the economically successful to hand over most of what they have earned to the state, and it is inappropriate to say of anyone who drifts in and out of work that he is lazy or irresponsible."

The primary fallacy of the Left's redistribution plan is that it does nothing to end the pattern of poverty. Robbing Peter to pay Paul does no good without rehabilitating Paul. I like the old saw that says if you give a man a fish you feed him for a day but if you teach him how to fish you feed him for a lifetime. The current system of welfare entitlements is the equivalent of giving the man a fish. It benefits no one but the charter members of the Victimization Industry, people like Jesse Jackson and Al Sharpton. The rationale for the welfare state is the perception that low-income Americans can't make ends meet without help. This would seem to imply assistance that is temporary until the recipient gets back on his feet. No such luck. "The problem is that Washington is building a culture of dependency," says CNN, "with ever more people relying on an ever-growing federal government to give them cash or benefits."

We need to recognize that the welfare entitlement

system is at odds with American values. "The intellectual underpinning of the welfare state," says Charles Murray, "is that human beings are not really responsible for the things they do." The welfare state has become a permanent, institutionalized solution to what should have been a temporary problem. Under our culture of dependency, welfare recipients lose the work habits and job skills that would otherwise make them independent. By providing a steady stream of income to unwed mothers, the system has eliminated fathers because payments are tied to their absence. Poverty is transferred from generation to generation with no hope in sight. "People feel trapped," said Sen. Rand Paul, "and it's not their fault, the government doesn't provide them an exit."

Thanks to the free market economy—not the welfare state—the poor in America are better off today than the middle-class of fifty years ago. "Poverty no longer has the resonance it had in the first half of the twentieth century," says Charles Murray. Leftist redistribution of income could never accomplish that, Thomas Sowell explains, because even if all the wealth of rich people was confiscated and redistributed, the status of the poor would not be improved. "Many attempts at redistributing wealth in various countries," Sowell points out, "have ended up redistributing poverty." Sowell's conclusion is that the agenda of the Left "does not really do much good for the poor, and some of that agenda actually makes the poor worse off."

Cultural Suicide

The purely economic drawbacks of the welfare system are dwarfed by the resulting cultural damage. "A significant and growing portion of the American population," says Charles Murray, "is losing the virtues required to be functioning members of a free society." In terms of survival, Murray argues that accepting responsibility is the most important value. Without it, he says, life has no meaning. The challenges of life are diminished. People lose the incentive to live their lives and they turn into robots.

When people receive free basics—food, shelter, and the like—from the government, it has a negative impact on other human needs. For example, says Murray, people need self-respect, but self-respect must be earned—it cannot be self-respect if it's not earned—and "the only way to earn anything is to achieve it in the face of the possibility of failing." With any accomplishment in life, he says, "responsibility for the desired outcome is inseparable from the satisfaction." So if you know that you got a promotion just because you're the boss's nephew, or because the civil service rules specify that you must get that promotion if you have served enough time in grade, or because you were the beneficiary of affirmative action, deep satisfaction is impossible. In other words,

> "All of these good things in life—self-respect, intimate relationships, and self-actualization—require freedom in the only way that freedom is meaningful: freedom to act in all areas of life coupled with responsibility for the consequences of those actions. The underlying meaning of that coupling—freedom and responsibility—is crucial. Responsibility for the consequences of actions is not the price of freedom, but one of its rewards. Knowing that we have responsibility for the consequences of our actions is a major part of what makes life worth living."

The ultimate question, according to Murray, is how can we provide support to people in a way that leaves them responsible for the consequences of their actions? This is consistent with my suggestion from *In Lies We Trust*: The way to solve the poverty crisis in black America is to replace the "give them free stuff" welfare mentality with programs that prepare low-income African-Americans for self-sufficiency. Unfortunately, many Americans have bought into the belief that poverty can be eliminated by throwing money at it. What else could account for the popularity of Bernie Sanders? There is no way of getting around it, people like free stuff. To believe this way is to fall for the leftist hoax, perpetuated by big government, that the answer to all our problems is a comprehensive redistribution of resources.

Black Privilege

No discussion of taking personal responsibility would be complete without examining what I call *black privilege*. In Chapter Two, I attempted to debunk the concept of white privilege. Whatever those privileges may have been in the past, they are no longer prevalent in today's America. "More whites have begun talking about themselves as a racially oppressed majority," reports CNN. "In a widely publicized 2011 survey, white Americans said they suffer from racial discrimination more than blacks."

In addition to being racist, white privilege constitutes an attempt to relieve minorities—especially African-Americans—of responsibility for the problems in their respective communities by placing the blame on a so-called tradition of white racism. The same justification is used for *Black Lives Matter*, a subset of the white privilege argument created by a small but vocal and violent cadre within the black community.

The Black Lives Matter platform is based on the contention that racist police and a biased justice system explain why a disproportionate number of black men are in US prisons. As substantiated by political commentator Heather Mac Donald, author of *The War on Cops*, this is an outright lie. Statistics clearly demonstrate that large numbers of black males are in jail because black males commit a disproportionately high percentage of all crimes. The police, says Mac Donald, are not the enemy. They are trying to protect blacks from criminals. Many blacks are begging for more cops on the streets of their neighborhoods. In fact, former FBI Director James Comey blamed BLM indirectly for the *Ferguson effect*, the idea that increased scrutiny of the police following the 2014 shooting of Michael Brown in Ferguson, Missouri, has led to an increased crime rate in the US.

According to Colin Flaherty, author of *Don't Make the Black Kids Angry*, BLM is a way of covering up the truth:

"A new generation of black leaders and white enablers want to remove black violence from the table and instead focus on the Big Lie: The war on Black People and how racist white people are waging it...That is the biggest lie of our generation. Because just the opposite is true. Black crime and violence against whites, gays, women, seniors, young people and lots of others is astronomically out of proportion."

Although BLM has received the support of many politicians including former President Obama, numerous critics—including yours truly—have accused BLM of anti-white and anti-rule-of-law radicalism. The violent core of BLM is exposed for all to see in the thuggish tactics employed by its supporters. "Rather than trying to persuade," says *The Atlantic*, "they're aiming to target skeptics, adversaries and even weak allies with shaming, verbal attacks, and attempts to silence them." In a further act of hypocrisy, anyone suggesting that "All Lives Matter" is immediately slammed by BLM supporters as racist.

Heather Mac Donald contends that the bottom line question is: Should African-Americans be held responsible for their own behavior—including criminal behavior, or are they victims of a racist society? Mac Donald and I are in agreement that blacks cannot shirk responsibility for their own behavior. The notion that African-Americans are victims of a racist society may have been true prior to the 1960s, but this is a half-century after the Civil Rights Movement. "White institutional racism has disappeared from our society," says Scott Greer in *No Campus for White Men*. "Black Americans now have every opportunity that white Americans have long enjoyed."

Actually, in today's America, the tables have turned. The oppression side of the racial equation has been transformed into a case for benefits. What we are witnessing now is *black privilege*. African-Americans are accorded special treatment across the board. "Victim status is treasured in America," says Ben Shapiro, "and black skin guarantees automatic victim status thanks to America's history." Being black today, Shapiro concludes, grants privileges ranging from landing coveted college scholarships to becoming activists who can build careers on racial grievances. Here are some examples of black privilege:

- Affirmative action quotas are the norm in education and employment—"more firmly entrenched in our society than ever before," says Scott Greer.
- Political correctness supports anything related to African-Americans and condemns anything related to Caucasian-Americans.
- College and university courses are specially designed

for black students.
- Black students benefit from the lower standards applied by college professors who practice "affirmative grading."
- Corporate diversity programs: CNN reports that corporations offer programs and internships to black workers but not to whites.
- Diversity training represents blacks in a positive light and whites negatively.
- Many courts are reluctant to prosecute blacks for various criminal acts in fear of being called racist.
- Blacks can belong to clubs and organizations that cater specifically to their race, reports CNN, "but there's no National Association for the Advancement of White People because such a group would be deemed racist."
- Media bias caters to positive depictions of blacks and avoids negative ones.
- "Black pride" is considered a form of empowerment; "white pride" is considered a form of racism.
- Blacks can get away with racial slurs, but whites can't use the N word.
- Hollywood casting has completely turned around as a consequence of aggressive lobbying by black special interests.
- Black privilege even extends to the White House, observes author David Horowitz, alleging that Obama "wouldn't be elected dogcatcher if he wasn't black."

The white establishment is bending over backwards to accommodate African-Americans who demonstrate even marginal capabilities. You won't see that happen in the NBA, which is based on performance, but the rest of our society has ceased to be a meritocracy. Given the enormous strides we have made on the issue of race, black privilege is no longer justified. Black privilege is just as racist as white privilege.

The Left is delighted with black privilege because it helps to destroy the important American value known as taking personal responsibility. Progressive liberals would rather see low-income blacks dependent on big government, believing that they are entitled to special privileges and yet trapped in the tentacles of the welfare state. Black privilege, in the long run, perpetuates the victim mentality. It is just not going to be good for anyone, regardless of skin color.

The Nanny State

We are fortunate to have a living laboratory in the European welfare state. After World War II, most of Western Europe bought into the idea that the state exists to take care of its citizens—literally. "It's a political system," says Bill O'Reilly, "that limits personal income through taxation in return for cradle-to-grave payouts from the governments." On the surface, it looks inviting. Most Europeans enjoy free healthcare, free education, long-term unemployment benefits, early retirement, long annual vacations, generous pension programs, childcare, and housing assistance. For example, a single parent with two children in Denmark could receive more than $38,500 in benefits.

Charles Murray calls this the *Europe Syndrome.* "The purpose of life is to while away the time between birth and death as pleasantly as possible, and the purpose of government is to make it as easy as possible to while away the time as pleasantly as possible... The idea of work as a means of self-actualization has faded."

Just as most things that seem too good to be true usually are, the European nanny state has a couple of serious drawbacks. The socialist paradises are beginning to run out of money. Fewer young people are available to subsidize the program. One way to deal with the declining birth rate is to import Third World immigrants who will pay taxes to shore up the revenue deficit. "Sooner or later," Murray warns, "the immigrants, too, will succumb to the incentives that the welfare state sets up. But the more immediate problem is that most of the new workers come from cultures that are radically different from those of Western Europe. In some cases, those cultures despise the values that led to the welfare state."

In order to survive, most of the nanny states are adopting austerity measures: higher taxes, raising the retirement age, cutting benefits. The whole apparatus is falling flat on its face. "The simplest way in which the advanced welfare state will lose attractiveness," says Charles Murray, "is the looming bankruptcy of the European welfare states."

The other drawback is a social and cultural one. The nanny state makes people lazy. The American virtue of self-reliance is not high on the European charts. The traditional continental work ethic was slowly replaced by a sense of entitlement, says *Brussels Journal*, "while the high taxation and the passivity bred by the system eroded initiative and the will to take risks." In Sweden, for example, people coming from a strong tradition of entrepreneurship and hard work were initially reluctant to take advantage of the system. Eventually they adapted their morality to maximize the available benefits. When people discover they can rely on government handouts, they lose their drive, initiative, and desire to work.

Another casualty of the nanny state is the institution of marriage, which is on the decline in Europe. "What is the point of a lifetime commitment," says Murray, "when the state will act as surrogate spouse when it comes to paying the bills?"

We are witnessing the same trends in the US thanks to Uncle Sam's welfare state. The federal government is growing rapidly in order to keep pace with entitlement programs. "As a result," says Cato Institute Senior Fellow Michael Tanner, "we are well down the road toward a crisis similar in scope to Europe's. It is only the size of the US economy and the dollar's status as the world's reserve currency that has staved off a major crisis. But that will not protect us forever."

Empowering Incompetence

In addition to shutting down free speech, political correctness empowers incompetence by members of protected groups. Based on their current level of ability, incompetent people often stay on welfare. Thanks to PC, you can't criticize them, and they have no incentive to take responsibility for their behavior by seeking self-improvement.

The satirical website *Onion* reported that the Senate is considering a bill sponsored by the Democratic Party called "The Americans With No Abilities Act." It is regarded as a major legislative goal, says the *Onion*, by advocates of the millions of Americans who lack any real skills and ambition. "Roughly 50 percent of Americans do not possess the competence and drive necessary to carve out a meaningful role for themselves in society," said a fictitious senator. "We can no longer stand by and allow People of Inability to be ridiculed and passed over. With this legislation, employers will no longer be able to grant special favors to a small group of workers, simply because they have some idea of what they are doing."

Supporters of the bill point to the success of the US Postal Service and the state Motor Vehicle Departments, which have a long-standing policy of providing opportunity without regard to performance. Under the new bill, more than 25 million mid-level positions will be created, with important-sounding titles but little real responsibility. Mandatory non-performance-based raises and promotions will be given to guarantee upward mobility for even the most unremarkable employees.

Finally, the Americans With No Abilities Act contains tough new measures to make it more difficult to discriminate against the non-abled by banning discriminatory hiring interview questions such as, "Do you have any skills or experience that relate to this job?"

"As a non-abled person, I can't be expected to keep up with people who have something going for them," said Helen Fournier, who lost her position as a lug-nut twister at the GM plant in Flint, Mich., due to her inability to remember "righty tighty, lefty loosey". "This new law should be real good for people like me. I'll finally have job security."

The Self-Made Man

Nothing epitomizes taking personal responsibility more than the story of Trump's National Economic Council Director, Gary Cohn. As a child with dyslexia, Cohn overheard a teacher tell his parents that he would be lucky to grow up to be a truck driver. Was he encouraged to avoid responsibility because of his condition? Did he blame his parents, or perhaps the society? Did Cohn wind up on welfare? In spite of his handicap, the truck driver-to-be managed to finish college. While working as an aluminum siding salesman, Cohn visited the commodities exchange in New York City and decided on the spot that he wanted a job on Wall Street.

Cohn had no background in finance nor did he have any

contacts in the financial world. His "white privilege" was nonexistent. What he did have was drive, courage, and the willingness to take risks. He went down to the floor of the commodities exchange and tried without success to gain entry. As he was outside looking in, Cohn did something extraordinary. He overheard a trader say to an assistant, "I'm going to La Guardia. I'll call you when I get to the airport." Cohn followed the man to the elevator where he said, "I heard you say you're going to La Guardia. So am I. Want to share a cab?"

As it turned out, the man ran the options business for a major Wall Street firm. Cohn did not even know what an option was but he didn't let that stop him. During the ride between Wall Street and La Guardia Airport, Cohn convinced his taxi companion to give him a job interview. He began working for the man a week later. Cohn, a kid from Cleveland with dyslexia, eventually rose to the presidency of Goldman Sachs and now is holding down an important job in the Trump administration.

That is an American story. We need stories like Cohn's. We need the myth of the self-made man. A country determines its direction by the myths it embraces. The Left wants to destroy Cohn's story in order to justify the aggrandizement of the nanny state.

Chapter Six
Dismissing the Rule of Law

An angry young woman, participating in a violent street demonstration opposed to the election of Donald J. Trump, informs a TV reporter that she will not allow Trump to take away her rights. On *Facebook*, another angry liberal writes: "We need to roll up our sleeves and be ready to remind [Trump] that we aren't going to sit back and surrender to his will. That we are strong and loud and our rights matter."

What rights, exactly, are they afraid of losing? The answer came in an opinion piece from the *San Francisco Chronicle*. After alleging that Trump wants to "break up our homes, assault us, wall out our families, and ban us from entering the country," the author fires her thunderbolt: Trump will "subject us to unspecified forces of law and order."

The author thinks the imposition of law and order will destroy the rights we enjoy as citizens. She believes that breaking a law you dislike is a right. Especially breaking the law by entering the country illegally. Many in the USA, particularly those of college age, have been indoctrinated to believe that the Constitution accords them the right to be "safe" from contradictory opinions and political viewpoints. If you disagree with them, you are taking away their rights.

DISMISSING THE RULE OF LAW

You are victimizing them.

Behind all the anti-Trump demonstrations is the desire of the protestors to be perceived as victims. Victims of the system. Victims of racism and sexism. Victims of anything at all just so long as they are entitled to be compensated for their victimhood. So what does it really mean to be a victim? A victim is a person who has come to feel helpless and passive in the face of misfortune or ill-treatment. The operative word is "passive," which implies that you do not have to be responsible for your own behavior if you ignore the rule of law. You can trash the streets in protest, set fire to cars and property, attack innocent bystanders—with no fear of reprisal. You are not responsible. It is all Trump's fault. He is responsible.

The victimhood argument fails because everyone is responsible for his actions. Yet victimization has become an industry in the USA. For this reason, it is not surprising that the post-election landscape was littered with victims strutting their stuff. We watched thousands of mostly young people marching down the streets and boulevards of our cities with a big chip on their collective shoulder. The person they wanted to be president lost the election. Their teachers told them they have a right to feel safe and now they feel unsafe.

Because these people are victims, they believe they have the right to deny others their rights. They have the right to tell you who to vote for. They have the right to disregard law and order at their pleasure. They have the right to free education, free healthcare, free living subsidies. They have the right to enter the country illegally and receive unearned benefits. There is only one problem. Everything has a cost, and the cost of denying the rule of law is chaos and anarchy.

The violent protestors are encouraged by a permissive, progressive society that encourages the values of the Left.

Let's be clear about this—the violent protestors are not victims. These people have made a choice and must be held to account. They are criminals and should be punished severely.

The Left wants to suspend the rule of law when it suits their purpose. Thanks to Obama's lawless behavior while in office, you can see it filtering down everywhere. On airplanes, passengers are violating important safety rules, placing other passengers at risk. Drivers are testing traffic laws to an extent never seen before on our streets and highways. Petty larceny and embezzlement by employees used to be the exception; now they are the rule.

Politicians are guilty of obvious corruption and no one seems to care. The Clintons have sold the country out to the highest bidders through their so-called foundation. Rep. Charles Rangel seems to be immune from having to pay his taxes. Rep. Maxine Waters has created her own self-serving canon of ethics.

California has passed Proposition 47, which reduced the classification of most "nonserious and nonviolent property and drug crimes" from a felony to a misdemeanor. As many as 10,000 inmates became eligible for return to the streets. If one of them should happen to burglarize your home, they will walk away if the value of stolen goods is under $950.

On college campuses, violence regularly accompanies protests against conservative speakers with little or no consequences for the perpetrators. They know they will not be prosecuted or even arrested. The attempt to shut down free speech by means of violence or the threat of violence is, in the words of Sam Harris, a "phenomenon of the Left." When we see videos of Occupy Wall Street, Black Lives Matter, or campus activists smashing windows and assaulting the police, we are witnessing the very essence of the Left. Unfortunately, the Left has been taken over by anti-free speech advocates for whom there is no moral compass. The end justifies the means. This is the ugliest manifestation of leftist politics. Violence can only lead to more violence. It is an express train to totalitarian rule and therefore a strong reason to reject the Left.

We are witnessing an era in which contempt is being shown for the law not only by citizens but also by a government that has refused to enforce its own laws. If we condone the disregard for one law, it sends a message that other laws can be similarly ignored. Here are some notable examples of contempt for the rule of law:

- The president (Obama) encouraging private citizens to break the law.
- Massive illegal immigration from south of the border.
- The federal government's refusal to enforce existing immigration laws.
- Sanctuary cities that choose to ignore immigration laws.
- Civil disobedience in the form of rioting, anti-police activism, and seizure of government property.
- A spike in the number of felonies reported by local law enforcement.
- Disregard for the US Constitution by elected representatives and appointed judges.

Revisiting the Constitution

"Why does the Constitution matter?" Mark Levin asks in *Plunder and Deceit*. The answer is that it provides the rule of law for a republic that protects our liberties from tyrannical control. Every "speck of liberty" we have, Levin says, comes from that document. In order to function without undue government interference, we need fixed rules that allow the individual to predict what the government will do in specific circumstances. Without the rule of law, the alternatives are totalitarianism or anarchy.

There is a major disagreement about how the Constitution should be interpreted. Conservatives believe in a strict adherence to the letter of the Constitution and the intention of the founders. The Left wants to dump the Constitution in favor of the "flavor of the month."

"I firmly believe the Constitution is a living document that evolves as our country evolves," says liberal Sen. Dianne Feinstein. The Supreme Court, she says, should engage in ongoing constitutional reinterpretation in accordance with contemporary perceptions of Supreme Court justices. This attitude can be traced back to Woodrow Wilson. He argued that the courts are not bound by the Constitution and that "governments have their natural evolution and are one thing in one age, another in another." Mark Levin says Wilson wanted to give the central government "unrestrained flexibility and freedom to operate where the rights of actual human beings are diminished and their pursuits restricted."

The danger is that without constitutional limits on the federal government's authority, individual rights are jeopardized. "The Constitution," says Levin in *Ameritopia*, "would become the vessel into which the utopians pour their agenda." The "living Constitution" could then be changed to suit the whims of the party in power. The rule of law would be whatever the tyrant in power says it is, which is how it works in North Korea. Levin's conclusion is that, "The 'living Constitution' is a constitution on its deathbed." The Supreme Court should not become a weapon in a class war against the successful and powerful, agrees David Horowitz. Hillary Clinton, had she been elected tyrant—excuse me, president—would have turned the Supreme Court into a leftist free-for-all with a bias in favor of big government vs.

individual rights.

Obama Strikes Again

One of President Obama's most heinous offenses was encouraging us to deny the rule of law. He used executive orders to bypass the other branches and set up an imperial presidency. "I think [the Constitution] is an imperfect document," he said, "This is a document that reflects some deep flaws in American culture." Obama's criticism of the Constitution apparently fueled his assumption of powers that were not delegated to the executive branch. In immigration matters, for example, Obama used executive orders to nullify core parts of existing law and substitute his own political preferences. When Congress did not act to adopt his immigration agenda, Obama decided to act on his own. He ordered the deferral of deportation of several million illegal aliens, assigning them temporary legal status.

In the domestic crime arena, Obama consistently encouraged disrespect for laws and the police. When police in Cambridge, Massachusetts, arrested black Harvard Professor Henry Louis Gates, Obama criticized the cops before the facts were in. The president implied that racist white police target innocent black men, a liberal canard. After the shooting of Trayvon Martin, a black teenager with a violent history, Obama enflamed racial hostility with his comment, "If I had a son, he'd look like Trayvon." Another poorly timed interference by the president. This time the public was manipulated into believing that the perpetrator was actually the victim. It led directly to riots and anti-police protests. Obama and Attorney General Eric Holder continued to push the leftist "cops are racist" propaganda, fueling further disrespect for the rule of law. What Obama's deeds all have in common is an attempt to distort the facts in support of the race card.

Obama continued his lawless reign by lying to the American public about his signature health care program. Before Obamacare, the right of Americans to choose their doctor and to choose their health care plan was part of the American social contract. "Obama and the Democrats were able to subvert both these individual freedoms," says David Horowitz, "only because they deliberately pretended that Obamacare wouldn't do just that. The same was true of the provision that provided health benefits to illegal aliens." The beans were spilled by Obamacare architect Jonathan Gruber, who admitted that the president had lied to the American public in order to expand government control over the individual. The real intention, says Horowitz, was for Obamacare to fail, and then to be replaced by a single-payer plan where the single payer is the US government. The single-payer option means a government agency would have access to all health and financial information of every American. "Unscrupulous government bureaucrats would have vital information about any individual to use as blackmail against political opponents," says Horowitz. "This is the basis not only for a socialist state but for a totalitarian one in which every individual is at the mercy of the rulers."

Obamacare was "blatantly unconstitutional," says Harvard Law graduate Ben Shapiro. "It was one of the worst violations of individual liberty in American history—the federal government was claiming the authority to punish you for failing to buy something they wanted you to buy." Commenting on the 5-4 Supreme Court ruling in favor of Obamacare, Shapiro calls it, "The worst kind of bullcrap ever put on Supreme Court paper."

The propensity of Barack Obama and Hillary Clinton to disregard the rule of law can be traced back to the influence of Saul Alinsky, a well-known leftist known as the father of community organizing. His book, *Rules for Radicals*, is the Left's handbook for achieving progressive goals. Alinsky agreed with the brutal advice in Machiavelli's famous treatise, *The Prince*, that "the end justifies the means."

> "The Prince was written by Machiavelli for the Haves on how to hold power," Alinsky explained. "Rules for Radicals is written for the Have-Nots on how to take it away."

Alinsky advised his disciples to join the Democratic Party in order to subvert America's institutions from within. It's the very same thing Alec Guinness does in *Dr. Zhivago* when the "party" orders him to join the army. Obama and Clinton did what they were told. To subvert American institutions, Clinton—who came dangerously close to the Oval Office—knowingly violated the Espionage Act, obstructed justice, and perjured herself. "How damaging is that to the rule of law," says David Horowitz, "and to the core idea that ours is a government of laws and not of individuals who can get away with anything if they have the right friends." Dinesh D'Souza and Martha Stewart went to jail for offenses that pale in comparison to Hillary's, yet Hillary was untouchable. D'Souza and Stewart didn't have the right friends.

The 28th Amendment

Nothing epitomizes disrespect for our laws more than the epidemic of illegal immigration together with internal defiance of US immigration laws. "If you think America should have secure borders and a legal process for immigration, as every other nation does—Mexico in particular," says David Horowitz, "you are immediately in danger of having a progressive label you 'anti-immigrant,' 'racist,' and 'xenophobic.'"

Every country has a right to protect its borders. Even if we wanted—as Hillary Clinton did—to allow everybody into the country, the effects of such a population tsunami on our economic viability and social structure would be catastrophic. That's why we have laws restricting immigration. No foreigner has an inherent right, says Monica Crowley, to live in the US without first going through the established legal channels. "If you disregard those laws, then you simply have no right to come and stay," she says. "But instead of properly enforcing that basic supposition, we've made illegal aliens a protected group, and we've put up with sanctuary cities, limited deportations and workplace enforcement, and an essentially open border."

The open borders policy has allowed terrorists and criminals to flood into the country, says Professor Edward J. Erler. When illegal alien criminals are deported, they easily return to commit further crimes. These criminals are enabled by sanctuary cities—cities that refuse to cooperate with federal authorities on immigration matters. They result in safe havens for illegal aliens involved in a variety of criminal enterprises. We would not have sanctuary cities were it not for the refusal by the Obama administration to enforce federal immigration statutes.

We are witnessing the rise of a new "right" which, if liberals had prevailed in the recent election, might have been glorified in the form of a constitutional amendment. It would read something like this:

> "The 28th Amendment: A state, city, or individual may choose which laws they wish to obey and which laws they wish to disregard without risk of legal consequences."

For example, let's say that the mayor of New York City decides that murder is no longer a crime. "If you commit murder in Chicago," the mayor might declare, "come to New York and you will not be prosecuted." Or let's consider the possibility, as hypothesized by Mark Levin, that anyone who commits murder will be exonerated if they are raising a family. "New Yorkers value the importance of family over all other considerations. If you commit murder in New York, you will not be prosecuted if you can demonstrate that you are raising a family."

Sounds completely insane, don't you agree? But this is exactly what is happening with sanctuary cities. The mayors of New York, Chicago, San Francisco, and many other cities have decided that they are not obliged to enforce federal immigration laws. Undocumented aliens will not be challenged by local law enforcement nor will such persons be turned over to federal authorities as required by law, even if that person is a felon. Sanctuary cities oppose Kate's Law, which would impose mandatory harsh sentences against undocumented immigrants who commit felonies. And why do they support the defiance of federal immigration laws? On the grounds that people who break these laws are trying to raise their families and we just can't destroy the sanctity of the family. *Hallelujah!*

A similar situation played out on Fox's *Tucker Carlson Show*. Carlson was expressing his disapproval of violent protests by illegal immigrants. His liberal guest defended the protests with the specious argument that because the illegals work hard, they have the right to protest violently. Taken to its logical conclusion, illegals who commit murder and rape should go free if they can demonstrate that they work hard. It is the flimsiest of justifications.

On the *O'Reilly Factor*, a guest argued that sanctuary cities are justified because immigrants contribute to our society. When it was pointed out that millions of immigrants are here illegally, the response was the usual doubletalk that sidesteps the legal issue altogether. The problem we face, like it or not, is that when it becomes acceptable to disobey one law, the door is opened for disobeying all laws. If you can enter the country illegally without consequences, then why can't you commit murder or any other crime without consequences?

Our elected public officials take an oath to defend our system of laws. It is irresponsible and criminal when they encourage disrespect for the laws they are sworn to defend. It all starts at the top. President Obama, reacting to the violent protests after Trump's election, refused to speak out against the violence. Instead, he actually encouraged people to continue to break the law. If the president can do this, why can't a mayor or a governor? A dangerous precedent is being set.

The solution for progressives is the 28th Amendment. Let's institutionalize anarchy. That may sound like a contradiction in terms, but anarchy is what we are going to have if the rule of law is ignored. We can't have it both ways. Either we are a country of laws or we are nothing.

The Hypocrisy of Mexico

An interesting headline appeared on *Yahoo.com*: *"Mexico fumes over Trump immigration rules as US talks loom."* The Mexicans reacted defensively when the Trump administration announced plans to deport illegal immigrants. Mexican Foreign Minister Luis Videgaray said his country would not accept the new US rules. "I want to say clearly and emphatically," Videgaray announced, "that the government of Mexico and the Mexican people do not have to accept provisions that one government unilaterally wants to impose on the other. We will not accept it, because there's no reason why we should, and because it is not in the interests of Mexico."

One would think Mexico has liberal immigration laws that make ours seem racist and xenophobic by comparison. Not even close. Get ready for an eye-opener. Here is a summary of Mexico's *General Law on Population*:

- Illegal immigration is a felony in Mexico. "A penalty of up to two years in prison and a fine of three hundred to five thousand pesos will be imposed on the foreigner who enters the country illegally." (Article 123)
- Immigrants who are deported and attempt to re-enter can be imprisoned for 10 years.
- Visa violators can be sentenced to six-year terms.
- Mexicans who help illegal immigrants are considered criminals. A Mexican who marries a foreigner with the sole objective of helping the foreigner live in the country is subject to up to five years in prison. (Article 127)
- Immigration officials must "ensure" that "immigrants will be useful elements for the country and that they have the necessary funds for their sustenance" and for their dependents. (Article 34)
- Foreigners may be barred from the country if their presence upsets "the equilibrium of the national demographics," when foreigners are deemed detrimental to "economic or national interests," when they do not behave like good citizens in their own country, when they have broken Mexican laws, and when "they are not found to be physically or mentally healthy." (Article 37)
- Federal, local and municipal police must cooperate with federal immigration authorities upon request, i.e., to assist in the arrests of illegal immigrants. (Article 73)
- Shipping and airline companies that bring

undocumented foreigners into Mexico will be fined. (Article 132)

It is significant to recognize, as *American Thinker* points out, "there is no green card, no food stamps, or pathway to Mexican citizenship." And "while we invite illegal immigration with jobs, service in the US military, driver's licenses, and discounted college tuition denied US citizens from another state, Mexico slams the door," says *Investor's Business Daily*. In fact, Mexico has deported more illegal aliens than we have. From January to December, 2014, Mexico deported 107,199 Central American immigrants, while the US only deported 104,688 illegal immigrants.

"How's that for irony?" said Ruben Navarrette on CNN. "It seems that Mexicans are no more keen on losing jobs to Guatemalans, Hondurans or Salvadorans than Americans are about losing them to Mexicans. There is no denying the hypocrisy of Mexicans who insist on a secure border to the south but would prefer a porous one to the north."

Another issue is, what options exist for Americans who want to work in Mexico? They must obtain a permanent work visa called an FM3. To apply for the FM3, you are required to submit the following notarized originals (not copies):

1. Birth certificate.
2. Marriage certificate.
3. High school transcripts and proof of graduation.
4. College transcripts for every college you attended and proof of graduation.
5. Two letters of recommendation from supervisors you worked for at least one year.
6. A letter from your local chief of police indicating that you have no arrest record in the US and no

outstanding warrants, and that you are "a citizen in good standing."
7. Finally, you must write a letter stating why there is no Mexican citizen with your skills and why your skills are important to Mexico.

If you protest any of the Mexican government's actions, you are committing a felony. So what the hell is going on here? "Why is our great southern neighbor pushing us to water down our own immigration laws and policies," asks *humanevents.com*, "when its own immigration restrictions are the toughest on the continent?" What is fair for them ought to be fair for us. If we emulated Mexico's laws, they would denounce us as racists. Actually, Trump's policies are minor league compared to Mexico's.

One of Trump's campaign issues was his insistence that the US should not sell itself out in relationships with other nations. "We've made other countries rich while the wealth, strength and confidence of our country has disappeared over the horizon," Trump said in his inauguration speech. Under Obama, the US lost sight of a basic truth in international relations: Every country has the right to protect its borders. Trump's intention is plain. He wants to enforce our existing immigration laws for two reasons: For the sake of law and order (the president's job is to enforce the law, something that Obama never understood) and to protect the homeland from terrorist incursions.

Pushing back against Trump is a minority special interest group that wants to throw out our immigration laws in favor of their interpretation of social justice. In many cases, elected officials are encouraging this manifestation of lawlessness. The *Los Angeles Times* reported this statement by California State Senate majority leader Kevin de León: "It has become abundantly clear," de León said, "that Attorney General

Sessions and the Trump administration are basing their law enforcement policies on principles of white supremacy—not American values." This is an example of the racist white supremacy argument being used by the Left to subvert an important American value, the rule of law.

I would put it to you this way: When a corrupt country like Mexico has the good sense to insist on the rule of law for its borders, why aren't we doing the same? If Mexican politicians want to play hardball, I have no doubt Mr. Trump can show them how it's done.

Chapter Seven
The Deep State: Unelected Bureaucracy

Much is being written about the "deep state" and the "shadow government." The media refer to what is called the "state within the state," a behind-the-scenes power elite that runs everything. Some conspiracy theorists point to Obama holdovers intent on sabotaging the Trump administration. "We are talking about the emergence of a deep state led by Barack Obama," said Rep. Steve King, "and that is something that we should prevent." Newt Gingrich may be closer to the truth. "Of course the deep state exists," Gingrich said. "There's a permanent state of massive bureaucracies that do whatever they want."

I agree. The real deep state is the huge unelected bureaucracy that represents the "big" in our big government. Consider this Internet posting describing a winter snowstorm:

> "As the storm hits, and hundreds of thousands of non-essential government employees are sent home, perhaps it's time we asked ourselves... WHY ARE THERE HUNDREDS OF THOUSANDS OF NON-ESSENTIAL GOVERNMENT EMPLOYEES??"

It's a terrific question. The answer is that, for the last 100 years, the Left—with the collaboration of the Right—has indulged its appetite for more and more government. "Politicians of both parties spent the better part of the 20th century disregarding the Constitution," says Professor Ronald J. Pestritto of the *Heritage Foundation*, "as they looked to have government step up to solve every conceivable human problem." From a nation in which corrupt politicians ruled with an iron fist through the time-honored system of patronage, we have progressed to one in which politicians exercise insufficient control. The administrative state makes most of the decisions with little direction from anyone. The inference is that real political power resides with unelected officials rather than with our elected representatives.

Over the years, Congress enacted broad legislation for supervising more and more facets of the American economy and society. Existing government couldn't handle it all, so Congress delegated power to a vast new network of bureaucratic agencies. Franklin D. Roosevelt had a field day with his New Deal agencies, including the National Recovery Administration (NRA), the Works Progress Administration (WPA), the Emergency Banking Act, and the Civil Works Administration (CWA). Lyndon Johnson followed up in the 1960s with the Great Society and War on Poverty. Some of the original programs are still with us: the Securities and Exchange Commission (SEC), the Tennessee Valley Authority (TVA), the Federal Housing Administration (FHA), the Social Security Administration, and the Federal Deposit Insurance Corporation (FDIC).

As more publicly financed benefits were voted in and as more people qualified for those benefits, Charles Murray explains, more bureaucracy became necessary to administer all of it. Now you have more people depending on government either for benefits or for their jobs in the bureaucracy. That adds up to more votes for bigger government. Anyone whose life depends on handouts is likely to vote for left-leaning political candidates. And that, of course, translates into the Democratic Party.

Obama's passive approach to illegal immigration and his virtual open borders policy, says Professor Edward J. Erler, "supplied a significant clientele for the administrative state as it seeks to extend its reach and magnify its power. As such, it has redounded to the benefit of the Democratic Party—the party that favors the growth and extension of administrative state power."

Of all the ways in which the Left is attempting to destroy America, its support for an enormous bureaucracy is one of the most successful. The power of the bureaucracy is beyond the reach of constitutional safeguards. Whenever Congress decides to add another function to the federal government, it manifests in the form of an increase to the already engorged bureaucracy. In *Ameritopia*, Mark Levin explains the inherent danger:

> "With the people denuded of spirit and exceptionality, dependent on the government for their welfare, the democracy gradually transitions into a powerful administrative state... As the administrative state grows, the vote is less effective and the individual is increasingly disenfranchised."

It's Alimentary, Watson

The federal government lives up to Ronald Reagan's amusing quip: "Government is like a baby," said Reagan. "An alimentary canal with a big appetite at one end and no sense of responsibility at the other." It has become America's largest employer, consumer, property owner, contractor, lender, insurer, and pension fund. Running this behemoth is expensive. Federal government expenditures as a percentage of gross domestic product (GDP) grew from a modest 3.4% in 1930 to an incredible 24% in 2010. The Congressional Budget Office predicts that federal debt will soon exceed 100% of GDP. Mark Levin cites *USA Today*'s estimate of total unfunded government obligations at $61.6 trillion, or $528,000 per household. Your bill will be arriving next week. (Just kidding, at least for now.)

The total number of government jobs—federal, state, and local—in the US as of October, 2016, was 22,235,000. That almost equals the number of jobs in the entire Fortune 500. The number of manufacturing jobs was 12,258,000. The number of government employees exceeds manufacturing workers by 9,977,000. In 1979, the number of government employees was 16,045,000. The current figure represents an increase of 6,190,000 or 38.6%. The current population of the US is roughly 320,000,000. One in 14 Americans work for some form of government bureaucracy. Narrow that down to adults only and the number is about one in nine.

Government employees, says Levin, receive average salaries and benefits that are twice those in the private sector. It is doubtful that they are twice as productive. The bureaucracy protects incompetence and drives up the cost of government. The public's perception is that government workers are generally inept. When describing the bureaucracy, negative terms are popular. They include: "excessive red tape and routine," "petty officials," "excessive concentration of power," and "getting caught up in the bureaucracy." Business author Gary Hamel writes in the *Harvard Business Review* that bureaucracy "is akin to Soviet-style centralization and is the enemy of resilience." It "shrinks our incentive to dream, imagine and contribute," says Hamel. It causes our organizations to "remain incompetent at their core."

I just received an amusing anecdote over the Internet. Before mounting a fishing expedition, a king asks his court meteorologist for a weather prediction. "No problem," says the expert. "The weather will be fine." As the king is proceeding to the fishing grounds, he meets a peasant on a donkey. "Get back to the palace, sire," says the peasant. "It will soon rain cats and dogs." The king decides to trust his highly-paid meteorologist instead of the peasant, but sure enough it rains cats and dogs. The king fires the expert and offers the job to the peasant. "I don't know anything about the weather," says the peasant. "I get my information from the donkey. If his ears droop, it means that it is going to rain." So the king hires the donkey, beginning the practice of hiring dumb asses to work in the most important positions of government.

Acting as a fourth branch of government, the bureaucracy issues thousands of rules and regulations that have the same authority as acts of Congress, yet are subject to virtually no oversight by our elected representatives. "The imperial bureaucracy has grown so powerful and arrogant that it doesn't even feel like answering questions," says *Breitbart*. "True accountability would interfere with the power of the State, so accountability is routinely evaded." Its regulations impact every aspect of our daily lives, including the food we eat, the vehicles we drive, the air we breathe, the places where we live and work, the movies and television shows we watch, the way we raise our children, how we brush our teeth, and how we make love. In 1900, a person could function perfectly well with hardly any interference from the federal government. Today it is inconceivable. The government in Orwell's *Nineteen Eighty-Four* monitors the individual's every movement using cameras installed in the home. If the Left is successful, that may be next.

Where Are They?

The federal bureaucracy employs 2,804,000 people, according to the most recent data compiled by the Bureau of Labor Statistics. The Defense Department alone employs more than 750,000 bureaucrats. During the height of World War II, that number was fewer than 100,000. How did we win? Could it be that the government actually functions more efficiently with fewer bureaucrats?

Here is a breakdown of the top 25 civilian federal employers as of 2013 (from the *Office of Personnel Management*):

1. US Postal Service: 584,027
2. Department of Veterans Affairs: 323,208
3. Department of the Army: 264,906
4. Department of the Navy: 194,923
5. Department of Homeland Security: 192,073
6. Department of the Air Force: 169,440
7. Department of Justice: 115,616
8. Department of the Treasury: 112,461
9. Department of Agriculture: 95,223
10. Other Defense Activities: 75,223
11. Department of Health and Human Services: 72,703
12. Department of the Interior: 71,543
13. Social Security Administration: 62,549
14. Department of Transportation: 55,288
15. Department of Commerce: 45,035
16. Department of State: 41,768
17. US Courts: 33,271
18. Defense Logistics Agency: 24,331

19. Corps of Engineers: 23,230
20. NASA: 18,001
21. Department of Labor: 17,187
22. Environmental Protection Agency: 17,002
23. Congress: 16,432
24. Department of Energy: 15,213
25. Tennessee Valley Authority: 12,612

All federal agencies must comply with applicable regulations in the *United States Code*, a labyrinthine document that consists of many thousands of pages. According to the *American Society for Public Administration*, "The results of bureaucracy may at times be disappointing. However, we need to bear in mind that bureaucracy is the only way agencies can cope with the complexity of the legislation and mission assigned to them."

The power of the bureaucracy has grown as Congress becomes more and more dysfunctional. As a practical matter, Congress has abdicated much of its legislative power to the bureaucracy. It exposes a class of politicians who are less knowledgeable than their predecessors about the intricacies of the issues they must vote on. Well-informed members of Congress wouldn't have to leave the details to civil service workers. It brings to mind Rep. Nancy Pelosi's infamous statement about Obamacare: "We have to pass the bill so that you can find out what is in it." On the other hand, legislators often find the bureaucracy useful as a place to hang the blame when something goes awry. It is, as we discussed in Chapter Five, a convenient way to avoid taking responsibility.

The really dangerous development, says *Breitbart*, is that our elected representatives and unelected bureaucracy are "so interested in making the State bigger and richer that they'll no longer countenance even token attempts at holding it responsible for its actions, because that would empower the people who want to make it smaller."

How the Deep State Works

For an example of how the bureaucracy functions as a "deep state," let's take a look at the 2013 scandal in which it was revealed that the Internal Revenue Service had discriminated against conservative organizations applying for tax-exempt status. Section 501(c)(4) of the Internal Revenue Code exempts certain types of nonprofit organizations from having to pay income tax. Many conservative organizations, including "Tea Party" groups, applied for tax-exempt status that still would have allowed them to engage in lobbying and other political campaign activities. The IRS deliberately targeted those organizations based on their names or political themes in order to deny their applications. During the period under investigation, 292 applications from conservative groups were chosen for scrutiny while only 6 liberal organizations were chosen. Accusations mounted that Lois Lerner, director of the IRS's "Exempt Organizations Unit," and others knew that IRS agents were targeting conservative groups for special scrutiny.

Was the IRS directed to handicap conservative groups as a politically motivated strategy? Although President Obama denied any involvement, the affair raised suspicions to the contrary. Lerner took the Fifth and a rash of resignations occurred—including hers—but no one was prosecuted. Even liberal news pundits were appalled:

- NBC's Chuck Todd: "This is outrageous no matter what political party you are."
- MSNBC's Joe Scarborough: "This is tyranny."
- ABC's Terry Moran: "A truly Nixonian abuse of power

by the Obama administration."
- MSNBC's Rachel Maddow: "There is a reasonable fear... that the kind of power the IRS has could be misused."
- NBC's Tom Brokaw: "It's time for action."

Numerous committees issued conflicting reports. The Republican report accused the IRS of targeting Tea Party groups for "politically motivated reasons." The Democratic report blamed "gross mismanagement" but declined to accuse the IRS of being political motivated. The FBI concluded there was not enough evidence to warrant criminal charges. The investigation continues as *Judicial Watch* issued a statement in April of 2017 that, based on newly discovered documents, there is a "smoking gun":

> "No wonder the IRS hid these records. These new smoking-gun documents contain admissions by the Obama IRS that it inappropriately targeted conservative groups."

Out of Control

The extent to which the bureaucracy is out of control is exemplified by the Environmental Protection Agency. With a budget exceeding $8 billion, the EPA issues more than 1,500 regulations annually. Ben Shapiro, in *Bullies*, describes a frightening example of the EPA's power. A couple purchased a $25,000 parcel of land in northern Idaho near Priest Lake. Their property did not abut the lake. When they began building a house on their land, the EPA accused them of polluting the lake even though their land contained no water. If the couple did not repair the alleged damage, the EPA threatened to impose millions of dollars in fines—as much as $75,000 per day for noncompliance. The couple sued the EPA and the case went to the Supreme Court, which ruled against the EPA. The Court accused the EPA of bullying and placing the property rights of Americans at the mercy of EPA bureaucrats. Unfortunately, this ruling has not put a stop to the uncontrolled activities of agencies like the EPA. How many thousands of cases never get to court because the victims lack either the will or the resources to mount an adequate defense?

The point of all this is that the federal bureaucracy functions as a shadow government. There is little or no oversight by the "real" government. In fact, the real government often uses the shadow government to accomplish dirty tricks. "Each new bureau and program stretches thinner the ability of citizens and their representatives to keep track of the government's activities and to correct failures and abuses," says the *Cato Institute*. "This problem has been called *political overloading*." The armies of bureaucrats, says Charles Murray, "take trillions of dollars, spend a lot on themselves, give back a lot of it to people who don't need it, and dole out what remains with all sorts of regulations and favoritism."

The IRS scandal is unusual because of its public exposure. The media regularly report on the activities of the executive branch and the Congress, but we are told very little about what goes on behind the closed doors of the various agencies that make up the federal government. Most of the clandestine activities of the bureaucracy go unnoticed. I think it is fair to say that those activities number into the thousands. Our lives are affected by actions of unelected bureaucrats whose power delegitimizes the ballot box. We didn't vote for these people, the Constitution does not bestow legitimate powers upon them, and yet they function with the approval of our elected representatives. "Beltway culture offers us soothing illusions of responsible government limited by our electoral power," says *Breitbart*, "but in truth, it's too big to monitor, too powerful to restrain, and it has more power to change us than we have to change it."

The Obama administration was able to push through much of its leftist agenda by delegating authority to bureaucrats like the ones at the IRS, who were only too happy to play ball. A complicit Justice Department under Obama appointees Holder and Lynch refused to file charges against miscreants like Lois Lerner. One hand washed the other.

Under Democratic Party rule, the public has been silent. It is perhaps because we have become accustomed to living under the boot of big government. "The administrative state has not yet extinguished America's love of liberty," says Professor Edward J. Erler, "although it surely has made significant inroads over the years as Americans have become inured to being bullied by bureaucrats of all stripes." All of these shadow activities work in favor of bigger and more powerful government. Tick off one more advantage for the Left as it takes America down.

Trump promises to "drain the swamp," which scares the daylights out of the bureaucracy. But his victory has not discouraged the Left from its onslaught. Using the deep state and the mainstream media, the Left continues to attack our liberties. If we don't put a stop to it, the result could be another civil war. Daniel Greenfield, Journalism Fellow at the Freedom Center, writes:

> *"The left is now openly defying the outcome of a national election using a coalition of bureaucrats, corporations, unelected officials, celebrities and reporters that are based out of its cultural and political enclaves. There are two competing governments; the legal government and a treasonous*

anti-government of the left. If this political conflict progresses, agencies and individuals at every level of government will be asked to demonstrate their allegiance to these two competing governments. And that can swiftly and explosively transform into an actual civil war."

Greenfield is referring to the battle that is developing between the Trump administration and the federal bureaucracy. Federal workers and their unions are nearly unanimous in their support of the Democratic Party. Bureaucrats are alleged to have donated 95% of their campaign contributions to Hillary Clinton, and most of them voted for her. According to the *Washington Post*, immediately after the election, career bureaucrats began their collaboration with Obama holdovers to find ways of obstructing Trump and his agenda. A big ruckus occurred when Sally Yates, who temporarily took over the reigns at Justice, refused to support Trump's immigration ban. I'm certain we will see more of this.

Leaking information was at the forefront of the resistance, as bureaucrats from the intelligence community reportedly were responsible for the leaks that torpedoed Gen. Michael Flynn. Attorney Jay Sekulow has warned of "an unprecedented bureaucratic coup undermining our security." He is referring to actions taken by the Obama administration just before it left office in order to encourage the bureaucracy to sabotage Trump. Two weeks before Obama stepped down, he changed the rules making it easier to share classified information among governmental agencies. This may have resulted in the mysterious leaks.

Bureaucrats can be effective when they want to bring down a politician. The civil service system gives most of them unparalleled job security. It takes a constitutional amendment to fire, demote, or suspend a bureaucrat. If they decide to throw a monkey wrench into Trump's agenda, it won't be easy to remove it.

All government employees take an oath to support and defend the Constitution. If our bureaucrats decide to violate their oath, don't expect any objections from the Left.

What to Do?

Are we to be forever at the mercy of the bureaucracy? The time has come to recognize that our government is based on federalism, which limits the scope of the central government and reserves the majority of government responsibilities for states and cities. Most of the existing federal programs are not authorized by the Constitution. And, according to the *Cato Institute*, the bureaucracy is plagued by waste and mismanagement, fraud, duplication of programs, and obsolete agencies.

Is it too late to fix the problem? Cato suggests that some programs ought to be terminated, others should be turned over to states and cities, and a few can be privatized. Programs on Cato's list of potential terminations include the Departments of Commerce, Education, and Energy; the Army Corps of Engineers; and the National Zoo. Another group of programs could be cut back: Department of Agriculture, Medicare, and Social Security. Programs such as Amtrak and the Postal Service could be privatized. A major program that ought to be run by state and local governments is highway construction.

But don't ask the Left for permission. You won't get it.

Chapter Eight
The Kafir's Dilemma: Sucking Up to Islam

Recently I emailed a couple of articles about Islamic terrorism to an old friend. My views were not mentioned, just a link to the articles. His response was shattering. "I reject all hate mail," he said. "Don't ever contact me again." I had been convicted by the Left of Islamophobia, a dislike of or prejudice against Muslims.

It seems that my former friend's wife's illness had been successfully treated by a Muslim-American surgeon. Therefore my friend was willing to overlook the facts about Islam and what it means to be a practicing Muslim. Because of his self-image as a tolerant, humane, freedom-loving American, he had no compunction about giving a free pass to an ideology that promotes murder, intolerance, misogyny, and totalitarianism. "The far enemy is political Islam," said Dr. Bill Warner, founder of the Center for the Study of Political Islam, "the near enemy is the apologist for Islam." This is the liberal hypocrisy that is enabling a dangerous, medieval cult to whittle away at Western civilization.

"Islamic supremacism could never have advanced so far

and so fast without its alliance with the left," observes Pamela Geller, author of *Stop the Islamization of America*. "The left traditionally aligns itself with the totalitarian ideology of the day, whether it was Stalinism, Communism, Maoism, or National Socialism. The left is all about control. Sharia is also all about control. The Sharia exerts total control over the people, which is the very thing that the left desires and demands." Here is the confluence of Islam and the American Left: Both seek the destruction of our values.

When liberals insist that we should be tolerant of Muslims, their tolerance is a one-way street. "They are concerned about the rights of thugs but not about the rights of citizens," says British political commentator Pat Condell, "especially women." "Should asylum be extended to the adherents of religions that do not recognize the free exercise rights of other religions?" asks Professor Edward J. Erler. The rational answer is NO.

Ironically, the Women's March on Washington was organized by a Muslim woman from Brooklyn. Pamela Geller put her finger on the hypocrisy: "Where are the feminists and women's rights groups fighting against clitorectomies, honor killings, gender apartheid, and the oppression and suppression of women in Islam?" says Geller. "They are guilty of silence and complicity."

The Left will do back flips in support of the Stone Age people who have committed more than 26,000 acts of terrorism since 9/11. Obama brought thousands of them into the US with no regard for the safety of our citizens. An outraged conservative posted this rebuke of liberal hypocrisy on *Facebook*:

> "Where are your voices when innocent people are getting hurt? Where is your condemnation of this ideology? Where is your ever-vocal 'moral courage'

when a thing that must be said does not fit with the easy, tribe-sanctioned, virtue-signaling, PC press release? You've truly lost my respect. Your belief system gets people killed."

The Left hopes you are one of the bleeding-heart liberals who want to open the doors to anyone from anywhere as long as they have a desire to emigrate to America. Facebook is full of posts that suggest we must admit Middle Eastern refugees on humanitarian grounds. We're Americans after all, the argument goes, so we have to show compassion for suffering. Progressive liberals believe they occupy the moral high ground. Does it ever occur to them that their Pollyanna viewpoint can easily lead to the destruction of everything we revere, that in the real world we have a duty to protect the homeland from attack? Interestingly, Muslim countries understand this problem better than we do. As noted by *Family Security Matters*, several Muslim countries recognize the link between Islam and terrorism and therefore refuse to accept Muslim refugees. If they did accept the refugees, the West would not be facing this huge problem.

"A US foreign policy that recommends absorbing unvetted Muslim refugees has been advocated as compassion," says Nonie Darwish, author of *Wholly Different: Why I Chose Biblical Values Over Islamic Values*, "but in fact it is gross negligence and reckless endangerment to US citizens, Western freedoms and democracy." Americans have forgotten about the monstrous evil that was 9/11. The memory of the thousands who were slaughtered on that day is being defiled by those who would open our doors to the human beings who were responsible. Pamela Geller describes the sick irony:

> "Here we are, years after it was raining bodies on

9/11, and we have Muslim footbaths in universities and airports. We have textbooks that read like a press release on Islamic history. We have Islamic anti-Semitism infecting the whole soul of the world. We have the mosqueing of the workplace and public school. We have the United States Treasury Department giving seminars on Sharia finance. We have a Muslim Brotherhood-linked Congressman. Our universities and our college campuses have become hotbeds of Islamic fundamentalism."

Do you think we should have more Muslim "refugees" in the US? Are you kind and tolerant? Here is the dilemma for kind and tolerant Americans:

(a) *Should we emulate Angela Merkel and the Germans, and demonstrate our humanity, by importing millions of suffering people from the Middle East?*
Or
(b) *Do we have a responsibility to defend the US against the threat to our nation's security from Stone Age people who want to kill us?*

The Left's answer to the above dilemma, option (a), exposes the weakness in their argument. It is the equivalent of choosing the second option in this question: Would you like a nice slice of apple pie, or would you prefer me to drive an icepick into your eye? The Left would make an argument that you are being selfish in wanting two eyes. After all, if I poke out one of your eyes, you still have another one, don't you? How many eyes do you need? An anonymous warning that has been circulating on the Internet puts the issue in perspective:

"It takes a special kind of lunatic to think that importing welfare recipients who want to kill us is a good idea."

Whether we acknowledge it or not, Islam is fighting a war against our civilization. "How hard is it to understand that radical Islamic jihadis have declared war on the West?" asks Raheel Raza, president of the Council for Muslims Facing Tomorrow and founding member of the Muslim Reform Movement. "In simple English," she says, "this means: they will find you and kill you wherever and whenever they can."

"Make no mistake," said Pamela Geller. "We are at war. Our mortal enemy has made no secret of its goal and stated aim: 'eliminating and destroying Western civilization from within and sabotaging its miserable house.' Muslims are working in the United States now to make sure that Islam dominates by destroying our Constitutional freedoms. How do I know that? Because they've told us."

By bringing in refugees from terror-infested areas of the Middle East, warns Nonie Darwish, we are sending a dangerous message to the Muslim world: "Citizens in the West are not even bothering to protect their free system from being conquered by sharia-lovers, so perhaps the dreams of the Caliphate are not that bad after all."

Three questions need to be answered before we can reach an intelligent decision about Muslim immigration to the US:

1. Is Islam a religion of peace that is protected under the Bill of Rights?
2. Are most Muslims peace-loving individuals who reject terrorism?
3. Does a ban on Muslim immigration violate our tradition as a nation of immigrants?

Question: Is Islam a religion of peace that is protected under the Bill of Rights?

Government policy in most Western countries is to promulgate the lie that terrorist attacks carried out in the name of Mohammed have nothing to do with Islam. "We are not at war with Islam," former President Obama declared. "We are at war with people who have perverted Islam." Is that true? Have the hard-liners in the Muslim world perverted their religion? The answer is no. What is often incorrectly described as "radical" Islam is actually mainstream Islam. Dr. Bill Warner, author of many books on Islam, explains that in Islam,

> "Humanity is not seen as one body, but is divided into whether the person believes Mohammed is the prophet of Allah or not. There is a division into believer and kafir (unbeliever). Kafirs can be tortured, killed, lied to, and cheated."

The Quran, Islam's holy book, says that the "kafir" must be: hated (40:30); mocked (83:34); punished (25:77); beheaded (47:4); confused (6:25); plotted against (86:15); terrorized (8:12); annihilated (6:45); killed (4:91); crucified (5:33); and warred against (9:29).

In case you still don't get it, A. Z. Mohamed, a Muslim born and raised in the Middle East, has confirmed what is contained in the Quran:

- *Islam does not recognize Judaism or Christianity as religions.*
- *Muslims are enemies of, and must fight, Jews and Christians.*

- *Muslims will never be satisfied until all people submit to the beliefs of Islam and the laws of sharia.*

Islam is not a religion of peace as the subversive Council on American-Islamic Relations (CAIR) would have us believe. It is rather:

1. A *religion of intolerance*, preaching openly from its holy book against the rights of women, homosexuals, Christians, Jews, and *anyone* who does not submit to Islam.

2. A *religion of jihad*: The Quran orders Muslims to conquer and subdue people of other religions until they are in a full state of submission to Islamic rule. The evidence consists of more than 26,000 terrorist acts committed in the name of Islam since 9/11.

Former Muslim Ayaan Hirsi Ali, in her book, *Heretic*, writes:

> *"It is foolish to insist, as our leaders habitually do, that the violent acts of radical Islamists can be divorced from the religious ideals that inspire them. Instead we must acknowledge that they are driven by a political ideology, an ideology imbedded in Islam itself. Let me make my point in the simplest possible terms: Islam is not a religion of peace."*

"There is an Islamic problem," says Mosab Yousef, son of the leader of the terrorist group Hamas. "They are killing in the name of Allah and humanity needs to stand against this danger. This danger is against the [evolution] of mankind." Yousef became afraid of Islam when he witnessed a Muslim woman send five of her children to die as suicide bombers. "I have seen death and I came from hell," he says. Islam, he insists, is an ideology from the seventh century that lusts for power. Saying that Islam is a religion of peace, Yousef argues, creates the perfect climate for more terrorism.

An argument has been made that Christianity, Judaism, and Islam have similar histories of violence. The difference is that while Christianity and Judaism experienced major reforms, Islam is stuck in its medieval practices. In the West, we used to burn people at the stake for disagreeing with church doctrine. Islam is in dire need of a series of reforms comparable to those instituted by Christianity in the sixteenth through the eighteenth centuries. Until that reformation occurs, we have a responsibility to defend our values from the encroaching threat posed by people who hate everything we stand for.

Donald Trump's position on banning Muslims from entering the US has drawn fire from those who regard such a step as inconsistent with the freedom of religion guaranteed by the Bill of Rights. First of all, people who are not American citizens cannot assert rights under the US Constitution. "By the terms of the Constitution, free exercise of religion is one of the privileges and immunities attached to *citizenship*," says Professor Edward J. Erler. "It can hardly be said to be possessed by all those who seek refuge in, or wish to emigrate to, the United States. As a sovereign nation, it is beyond dispute that the U.S. has plenary power to determine the conditions for immigration."

Second, what does freedom of religion mean? Can any ideology qualify for benefits under this umbrella or does it have limits? You bet it does. Especially when the group in question is a totalitarian nightmare hiding behind the mantle of religion. "We have to stop pretending that Islam is a religion," said Dutch parliamentarian Geert Wilders. "The constitutional freedoms of religion do not apply to an ideology. Islam is a totalitarian ideology that aims to conquer the West. A free society should not grant freedom to those who want to destroy it."

Wilders has struck at the core of the controversy. Is Islam a religion or an ideology? My view is that Islam is a totalitarian political ideology cloaked in the disguise of a religion, which allows it to get away with murder—literally. When the power centers of the Islamic world cite the Quran to advocate *and in fact demand* the brutal murder of anyone whose behavior is deemed *offensive*—a code word for anyone who denies the core beliefs of Islam—then we are no longer dealing with a religion. Now what we have is a murder cult, and there is nothing in the Bill of Rights that supports this. "Let's not be politically correct about it," said Ayaan Hirsi Ali. "Violence is inherent in Islam. It's a destructive, nihilistic cult of death. It legitimates murder."

As Geert Wilders said, we cannot allow ourselves to be duped into granting freedom to those who want to kill us. Here is a relevant excerpt from my book, *In Lies We Trust*:

> "Thuggee was a murder cult in 19th century India that worshipped the Hindu goddess Kali. Each thug (hence our word for hoodlum) was given a strangling cord so he could murder as many people as possible in the name of Kali. (Remember the movie, Gunga Din?) The thugs succeeded in killing as many as 30,000 people a year until the British put a stop to it. All of a sudden freedom of religion implies a frightening possibility: the Thuggee should be accorded the freedom to worship their religion. Yet who would dare to suggest such an outrage? And the central question: Is there a difference between the behavior of the Thuggee and the behavior of radical Muslims? I don't believe there is."

If we cannot accept Thuggee as a religion deserving of constitutional protection, how can we do so for Islam? But Pamela Geller advises against claiming that Islam is not a religion. Her reason is strictly a pragmatic one: When opponents of a mega-mosque in Tennessee made this claim, the Muslim-appeasing Obama federal government intervened to insist that Islam is entitled to First Amendment protections. This is how the Left places all of us at risk. We must be prepared to act against those who would destroy America and American values. We have sedition laws that make it a crime to advocate the violent overthrow of the US Government. Is anyone paying attention? When intolerance and acts of violence are demanded by radical imams in Brooklyn, Chicago, and Sacramento, it is time to remove the blinders and recognize that freedom of religion does not apply.

Question: Are most Muslims peace-loving individuals who reject terrorism?

In yet another attempt to mislead the American public, Obama alleged that 99.9% of Muslims reject Islamic terrorism. In fact, a number of respected polls provide ample evidence that as many as 80% or more of Muslims worldwide agree with and support the most barbaric acts of the extremists. The *Gallup* poll classified one in three Muslims worldwide as political radicals who believe the terrorist attacks of 9/11 were completely justified. Do the math. One third of 1.5 billion Muslims amounts to half a billion radical Islamists. The *National Review* concluded, "When a position is held by one in five, one in four, one in three, it's part of the mainstream."

Hundreds of millions of followers are invested with the

imposition of universal sharia (Islamic law) and the murderous worldview that goes with it. The evidence demonstrates that the most barbaric ideas and practices—killing apostates, killing Christians and Jews and gays, subjugating women—are fundamental to mainstream Islam.

But what about the millions of Muslims who are not terrorists and who do not follow the radical imams? As in other religions, many people identify as Muslim for ethnic or social reasons. They do not follow the teachings of the Quran. These people simply want to live in peace. Can they be held accountable? There is a cogent answer to this question: They and other Muslims who might be described as "moderate" have been marginalized by their willingness to accept the rule of the hard-liners. Most of the German people during the Hitler regime were not Nazis, but by their silence they acquiesced to Nazi domination. The same was true of the silent Russian majority during the Stalinist period when 20 million people were murdered, and of the silent Chinese majority during the Maoist reign when 70 million Chinese were killed. The silent Muslims are irrelevant by virtue of their silence.

Question: Does a ban on Muslim immigration violate our tradition as a nation of immigrants?

President Trump has been under fire for wanting to impose a ban on immigration from a list of Muslim-majority countries. Liberals argue that we are a country of immigrants so we should not close our doors to Muslims, regardless of the threat posed by Islamic terrorism. Barack Obama and Hillary Clinton wanted to import millions of so-called Muslim refugees. The argument against this self-destructive policy can be found in the European experience. "One only has to observe the results of the refugee crisis in Europe to see what is in store for the American homeland," says Professor Edward J. Erler. Many countries in Western Europe—Germany, France, the UK, Belgium, Holland, Denmark, Sweden—have opened their borders to an avalanche of immigration from the Middle East. The results have been devastating in terms of crime, terrorism, drain on welfare budgets, and the assault by Muslim immigrants on the cultures of their host countries.

FrontPage Magazine reports that in Sweden with "a major increase in rape cases paralleling a major increase in Muslim immigration, the wages of Muslim immigration are proving to be a sexual assault epidemic by a misogynistic ideology. Statistics now suggest that one in every four Swedish women will be raped." In Cologne, a thousand Middle Eastern men groped and raped women in an orgy of terror. Ironically, German Chancellor Angela Merkel has invited more than a million of these "peaceful" people to live in her country. An entire nation's quality of life has been destroyed completely. German women are afraid to walk in the streets alone for fear of being raped by Muslim immigrants. Quaint German villages with a population of 2,000 have been forced to accept 1,000 male refugees from the Middle East. Those villages will never be the same again. The German government does not want you to be aware of the facts but it should not be a surprise to anyone who is paying attention.

> *"Germans have been warned that it is their duty to accommodate themselves to newly arrived refugees and not to place politically incorrect demands upon them—that is, not to demand that the refugees adapt to German ways,"* says Professor Erler. *"Some have advised German women in particular that if they don't wish to be harassed by male refugees, they*

should cover their heads and be accompanied outside of the home by a male. Will this be a part of America's politically correct future?"

As I am writing this, the news has just come through that more people have been killed in a crazed Muslim terrorist attack in London. The mayor of London, who happens to be Muslim, has declared that this is the "new normal." Theresa May, the British prime minister, made a point of affirming that Islamic terrorism is "a perversion of a great faith." Insane. The British are accepting jihad instead of fighting for the survival of their vibrant culture. The UK is becoming a nation of ghettos, said *Daily Mail* columnist Katie Hopkins on the *Tucker Carlson Show*. Evidently it has become more offensive to be anti-Muslim, Carlson noted, than it is to be anti-British.

Czech President Milos Zeman is one of many Europeans who believe it is not realistic to expect the integration of Muslims into Western society:

> "The experience of Western European countries which have ghettos and excluded localities shows that the integration of the Muslim community is practically impossible. Let them have their culture in their countries and not take it to Europe, otherwise it will end up like Cologne."

Pat Condell, as always, hits center target:

> "Germany's first female chancellor has made her country and Europe significantly more dangerous for women in order to accommodate an army of hostile third world misogynists. As a result, our society is now measurably less safe and less civilized and the rights

of women are effectively negotiable."

The Left wants to do to the US what Angela Merkel has done to Germany. Is this what we want to import to towns and villages across America? Do we want to sentence American women to the intolerance of Islam? The desire by American politicians to bring in Stone Age immigrants is "insane," says Professor Erler. "What other explanation could there be for the insistence of so many of our political leaders on risking the nation's security." In light of what we see in Europe, one might even say they are willing to commit national suicide by admitting refugees who want to kill us.

We cannot expect people from the Stone Age to be transported to a Western country and automatically be assimilated into the value system of that country. You can't put a Muslim man from Syria on a jet airplane that lands a few hours later at JFK Airport in New York City and expect him in an instant to shed his seventh-century Islamic mentality in favor of American values and customs. But that is precisely what progressive liberals want to do. It is precisely what President Obama was doing for eight years and what Hillary Clinton would have done had she been elected president. If Hillary had won, we would have hordes of unvetted Muslim immigrants pouring across our borders.

Let's consider what happens when Muslims come to the US as "refugees" from the Middle East. As in Europe, they immediately circle the wagons by forming Muslim enclaves that reinforce their unwillingness to assimilate. In France, Holland, and Sweden, these enclaves have been given the name "no-go zones" because police and fire departments are afraid to enter. This may be happening as we speak in parts of Dearborn, Michigan, and other American communities with high concentrations of Muslim immigrants. According to *Family Security Matters*, "Newly arrived Somali immigrants have transformed small towns and cities throughout the United States into *tuulas* (Somali villages). The process is underway in such places as Lewiston, Maine; Shelbyville, Tennessee; St. Cloud, Minnesota; Clarkston, Georgia; and Jamestown, North Dakota." As Muslim immigrants collect generous welfare benefits from our government, an attitude of hostility is directed at their host country.

While it is true that we are a country of immigrants, the current situation is very different from anything we have faced in the past. Historically, immigrants did not arrive on our shores with the intention of destroying our values and our civilization. On the contrary, they wanted to become Americanized. They wanted to speak English and to "fit in." They wanted their children to be Americans. America was a melting pot. None of this applies to Muslim immigration. Instead of assimilating and adopting American values as past immigrants did, Muslim immigrants to the US want to impose their values on us. They want us to assimilate.

As the percentage of Muslims in our population grows (the Muslim population increases geometrically because Muslims have battalions of children), more demands will be made to achieve Muslim dominance. Our Muslim guests want sharia law to replace American law. Free speech will end under Islamic blasphemy laws. Blasphemy and apostasy will be punishable by death. Our women must surrender all the gains made in the past half century of feminist activism by acknowledging that they are second-class citizens. If your husband wants to beat you, that is his prerogative. Polygamy should be accepted, along with female genital mutilation. Alcohol will be forbidden. The LGBTQ community will once more be forced underground. An epidemic of anti-Semitic atrocities will have to be overlooked by our law enforcement agencies.

The constant monitoring of American citizens in the

name of detecting terrorism will transform the US into a security state where individual rights will be sacrificed to the constant threat of terrorism. "Sacrificing liberty will be the price Americans pay to accommodate refugees," says Professor Erler. "In other words, it is the sacrifice we must make on the altar of political correctness."

The religious and political centers of the Muslim enclaves are mosques, often funded by extremist Wahhabi Muslims from Saudi Arabia, in which anti-Western doctrines are preached. Ilana Mercer points out:

> "Members of the crème de la crème of the American Muslim community routinely masquerade as moderates—pillars of the community—while in private and from their pulpits often advocating violence, advising their followers to work to impose the strict Islamic code of shari'a in the U.S., and swearing allegiances to al-Qaeda's capo di tutti capi."

When ex-Muslim Nonie Darwish visited mosques in the US, she witnessed first-hand how the imams are urging their Muslim congregations not to assimilate. The Center for Religious Freedom, as reported by Pamela Geller, found that Islamic supremacism, together with hatred of Jews and Christians, is taught extensively in American mosques. The Mapping Sharia project found that three out of four American mosques preach hate and incitement to violence. "They don't want to live in Muslim countries," said author and political commentator Ann Coulter, "and yet they want to change the non-Muslim countries they move to [into] Muslim countries."

Peter Hammond, in *Slavery, Terrorism, and Islam*, describes what has happened where Muslim immigration has grown as a percentage of the total population:

"When the population reaches 5% they exert influence disproportionate to their numbers, becoming more aggressive and pushing for Sharia law. When the population hits the 10% mark Muslims become increasingly lawless and violent. Once the population reaches 20%, there is an increase in rioting, murder, jihad militias, and destruction of non-Muslim places of worship. At 40%, there are "widespread massacres, chronic terror attacks, and ongoing militia warfare." Once beyond 50%, infidels and apostates are persecuted, genocide occurs, and Sharia law is implemented. After 80%, intimidation is a daily part of life along with violent jihad and some state-run genocide as the nation purges all infidels."

Trump's Ban vs. Rogue Leftist Judges

In response to these facts, President Trump issued two Executive Orders requiring a temporary ban on immigration from a short list of Middle Eastern countries. Federal District Court judges issued temporary restraining orders (TROs) that invalidate both presidential orders. The judges claim that the ban discriminates on the basis of religion and national origin. A three-judge panel from the 9th Circuit Court of Appeals refused an appeal to reinstate the ban. Although they have no authority to do so, a handful of liberal judges have effectively shut down the executive branch of the federal government.

The air is beginning to clear. Five judges from the 9th Circuit Court of Appeals have issued a dissent that refutes the legal basis for the District Court rulings. This opinion is not binding on the present case but it does forecast a big win for the administration. The five Court of Appeals judges hope that the administration will continue to appeal the District

Court rulings so they can be overturned. I am optimistic that the ban will soon be in effect.

The dissenting five-judge panel referred to the District Court decisions as full of "manifest" and "fundamental" errors. What follows is a breakdown of the panel's opinion in everyday English for the benefit of the average reader who has not attended law school.

1. The temporary restraining orders violate existing rulings by the Supreme Court and the Circuit Court of Appeals. The precedents say that so long as there is one bona fide reason for the president's action, it is not reviewable by the courts. If a reason is given by the president, a judge cannot overturn an Executive Order because he does not agree with the reason. In this instance, the countries identified by the president had all been previously identified by either Congress, the Secretary of State, or the Secretary of Homeland Security as areas of concern because of terrorist activity. "The President's actions might have been more aggressive than those of his predecessors," the dissenting opinion declared, "but that was his prerogative."

2. In addition to ignoring legal precedents, the District Court rulings ignored the applicable statute, section 1182(f) of title 8, that gives the president power over immigration. That statute states quite clearly that:

> "Whenever the President finds that the entry of any aliens or of any class of aliens into the United States would be detrimental to the interests of the United States, he may by proclamation, and for such period as he shall deem necessary, suspend the entry of all aliens or any class of aliens as immigrants or

nonimmigrants, or impose on the entry of aliens any restrictions he may deem to be appropriate."

3. A recent ruling from the Court of Appeals affirms that the president's ban does not discriminate against Muslims based on their religion. The reason: non-Muslims from the designated countries are subject to the same restrictions as Muslims. If a Christian from Yemen tries to enter the US, he falls under the same ban that applies to Muslims from Yemen. And even if it is a ban on Muslims, the courts still cannot challenge the president's decision:

> "Even if we have questions about the basis for the President's findings—whether it was a 'Muslim ban' or something else—we do not get to peek behind the curtain."

4. Claiming that foreigners have first amendment rights is contrary to Supreme Court rulings. The court has held that due process and equal protection do not apply to non-US citizens. Persons in the US cannot claim a constitutional right for foreigners to travel to the US.

5. A judge cannot demand that the president produce classified information to explain his decisions. The Supreme Court has ruled "the President does not have to come forward with supporting documentation to explain the basis for the Executive Order. The government may provide more details 'when it sees fit' or if Congress 'requires it to do so,' but we may not require it."

More to the point, the five justices have exposed the destructive tendency toward overreaching by liberal members of the judiciary.

"Whatever we, as individuals, may feel about the President or the Executive Order," the panel stated, *"the President's decision was well within the powers of the presidency... We cannot let our personal inclinations get ahead of important, overarching principles about who gets to make decisions in our democracy."*

A survey by Rasmussen Reports found that 68% of Americans support the president's order and believe the courts should abide by legal precedents and the Constitution. The rejection of Trump's travel ban is an example of how the leftist judiciary ignores the law in order to play politics. The "results-oriented judges" who stopped the ban, says attorney Robert Barnes in *Law Newz*, have not only shown contempt for the rule of law, they have attempted to reverse the outcome of the presidential election. My hope is that the dissenting opinion represents a movement by the judiciary to reform itself.

Meanwhile, what did the Obama administration do to counter the threat from Islam? The entire Middle Eastern region has been destabilized because of Obama's passivity. He did it deliberately. Then he opened the floodgates of unvetted immigration and relied upon laughable airport scrutiny that has yielded no useful results. According to *Investor's Business Daily*, Obama unilaterally eased immigration requirements for foreigners linked to terrorism, removed more than 4,000 suspects from the US terror watch list, and closed the borders to Christians fleeing persecution by Muslims.

The biggest fiasco was Obama's ban against racial profiling by our police, FBI, and homeland security agencies. Because "FBI headquarters refused to engage in racial profiling," said Ann Coulter, they failed to uncover the 9/11 plot. "The FBI allowed thousands of Americans to be slaughtered on the altar of political correctness." The New York City Police Department's counterterrorism unit, charged with detecting terrorist activity by carrying out surveillance of Muslim groups, was ordered shut down by a liberal mayor who happens to be Obama's ideological cousin. Mayor De Blasio's concern for protecting New York's citizens was clearly not as high a priority as his fear that the special unit would be considered Islamophobic. "The Boston Marathon bombers, the San Bernardino and Orlando killers were on the FBI's radar before their attacks," says David Horowitz, "but slipped off because of the prohibitions against taking their religious commitments and associations into account."

Obama and De Blasio typify the Left's connection with Islamic causes. We have evidence that the Muslim Brotherhood and other Islamic supremacist organizations have infiltrated our government at all levels. Obama followed to the letter the recommendations of Muslim groups, including de-emphasizing military anti-terror efforts in the Islamic world.

Islamophobia: Wolf in Sheep's Clothing

Which brings me to another dicey topic, Islamophobia. "Islamic law," explains Pamela Geller, "considers any critical examination of Islam to be blasphemous and subject to the death penalty." The term *Islamophobia* was invented by a front group of the Muslim Brotherhood as a weapon to stigmatize and silence Western critics of Islamic extremism, and to enforce Islamic blasphemy laws. "The trick," says Geller, "is to portray 1.5 billion Muslims as victims." Islamophobia is classic political correctness. If it prevails, we become infinitely more vulnerable to terrorism because we are afraid to talk about it. As I point out in my book, *In Lies We Trust*:

> "The thrust of the Islamophobia strategy is to (a) accuse Americans of harboring a deep prejudice against Muslims, (b) convince the public that, as a result, Muslims are disproportionately targeted by perpetrators of hate crimes and acts of discrimination, and (c) suppress any and all criticism of Islam and Muslims."

The truth is that hate crimes against Muslims have declined since 9/11 and constitute only a small fraction of overall hate crimes. The late author Christopher Hitchens reminded us that criticism of religion is protected under the First Amendment. Referring to Islamophobia as "religious bullying," Hitchens said, "We have to hear propaganda in the Muslim world telling children to kill Jews, Christians, and Hindus. That homosexuals should be stoned. And we have to claim not to be offended."

What offends me most about Islamophobia is the intention to curb free speech. And it is working. After the brutal San Bernardino terrorist attack, Attorney General Loretta Lynch threatened to prosecute anyone guilty of what she called "anti-Muslim rhetoric." Under the Obama administration, Muslims became a protected class. "All Americans must think and say only nice things about Islam," said journalist Matthew Vadum.

The United Nations has become a vehicle for the recognition of Islamophobia. Muslim states account for 18 of the 47 seats on the UN Human Rights Council. This Muslim bloc has been the driving force, says *cnsnews.com*, behind two key items on the Council's agenda: the campaign for anti-blasphemy laws and condemnations of Israel. Now it seems they have the support of UN Secretary General Antonio Guterres. Pamela Geller says Guterres "is a tool of the Organization of Islamic Cooperation, which has been running a years-long campaign against freedom of speech at the UN." Guterres has cited "Islamophobia" as the reason for increasing terrorism around the world. "One of the things that fuel terrorism," said Guterres, "is the expression in some parts of the world of Islamophobic feelings and Islamophobic policies and Islamophobic hate speeches."

WorldNetDaily argues that "Guterres just gave a free pass to Islamic extremists to commit acts of terror throughout the world." It's a lot like blaming the victim, says Phillip Haney, author of *See Something Say Nothing*. "He's giving them an out. If they're not required to take any responsibility for their terrorism and can simply blame the Islamophobic Western world," says Haney, "it's only going to get worse."

"Guterres is doing the bidding of Islamic jihadists and is advancing Islamic conquest by silencing truthful speech about Islam," former Congresswoman Michelle Bachmann told WND. "No other religion enjoys such protection from criticism," Bachmann said. "Ironically, no other religion in current times has advanced more violence, carnage and bloodshed than Islam and yet Islam's gatekeepers demand their religion not be criticized. We need to recognize this is nothing more than a well-designed strategy to achieve Islamic conquest and the UN Secretary General is now the jihadist's advocate."

For my money, you can't get more un-American than Islamophobia. Islamic values represent an absolute contradiction to ours. The two systems cannot coexist. Wherever Islam gains a following, Muslims demand an end to human rights and the freedoms that are taken for granted in the West. "Resist it while you still can," warned Christopher

Hitchens, "and before the right to complain is taken away from you which will be the next thing. You will be told you can't complain because you're Islamophobic."

We can't have it both ways. "For a democracy that believes in freedom, peace, and prosperity," said Secretary of Defense James Mattis, "the idea that this level of evil can exist is incompatible with our view of what we would like to see as we turn over this world to our children."

All Americans should be Islamophobes. One group in the US actually approves of the Islamophobia scam. According to a poll by Wenzel Strategies, 58% of Muslim-Americans believe criticism of Islam is not protected free speech under the First Amendment. "To learn who rules over you," said Voltaire, "simply find out who you are not allowed to criticize."

Chapter Nine
A Culture of Lies

In a totalitarian state like North Korea, functionaries wait to reveal their views until the party line has been articulated by leader Kim Jong-un. Once a lie has been formulated, the word is spread quickly among the faithful. Then they become disciples of *groupthink*. The American Left does the same thing. Groupthink, a term coined by social psychologist Irving Janis (*Visions of Groupthink*, 1972), occurs when a group follows the word of its leader and discourages dissent. The lack of individual decision-making relieves group members of having to take personal responsibility for their views. The key word for groupthink is conformity.

When your decisions are based on a party line rather than your own judgment, you have surrendered your mind to groupthink. In the US, the surrender is usually to the Left. I see this all the time on *Facebook* when people criticize conservative viewpoints without giving reasons in support of their position. It seems clear that they are spouting something they were told or something they heard on CNN. Many of the liberal guests on the *Tucker Carlson Show* do the same thing when Carlson challenges their position. Every time Carlson demands an explanation, they hem and haw and then repeat their original groupthink statement. Barack

Obama made good use of this concept when he ran for president in 2008.

Hope-a-Dope

Boxer Muhammad Ali had a slogan called "rope-a-dope" where he would dupe his opponent. By pretending to be trapped against the ropes, Ali would tire out the other fighter and then come back to win the bout. Candidate Obama used the concept of hope in a similar way in order to dupe the American voting public, composed of millions all too willing to surrender their minds to groupthink. I call his gambit "hope-a-dope." Obama won the presidency with his brilliant campaign slogan, "Hope and Change"—brilliant not because of what it meant, but rather because of what it did not mean. All by itself, "Hope and Change" doesn't mean a damn thing. Obama's slogan was a lie on purpose.

Hope-a-dope was intended to seduce gullible voters who were fed up after George W. Bush's second term in office. Hope and change. Change and hope. You could go along with it but you couldn't attack it because there was no "it." What would you say? "I am against hope and against change!" You would wake up in Bellevue wearing a straitjacket. Everyone wants hope and change. For millions of voters, it did not matter what Obama meant by hope. They voted for him because of what *they* thought it meant, not because of what *he* thought it meant. In other words, the whole campaign was a dirty trick.

The extent of Obama's lies is just beginning to surface. We know, for example, that Obama lied when he told us that he got rid of Syria's chemical stockpile. He lied when he said that the global war on terror is over. "On ethics," says Monica Crowley, "Obama told us that he'd lead the 'most transparent administration in history' and a new era of 'accountability.'"

Instead, he "stonewalled every investigation from Solyndra to the New Black Panther Party voter intimidation case to his own murky background to Fast and Furious."

His biggest lies were reserved for Obamacare. Obama told us that his health care program would help to improve the economy, lower costs, and deliver greater accessibility. And "if you like your plan, you can keep your plan." Instead, Obamacare torpedoed job creation, premiums have skyrocketed, millions lost their plans, and millions are still not covered by insurance. The Democrats love the higher costs of healthcare due to Obamacare because it will create greater dependence on government handouts, and therefore increase the number of people voting Democrat. Thank you very much.

Enter Donald Trump. Trump's election is a rejection of Obama's concept of hope, which reflects the leftist desire to minimalize all things American. Trump stands for the hopes and dreams of all those who were left out by Obama's anti-American platform. In an attempt to spin this around, Michelle Obama said that Trump's election is the destruction of hope. "See, now, we are feeling what not having hope feels like," Mrs. Obama told Oprah Winfrey. "Hope is necessary. It's a necessary concept and Barack didn't just talk about hope because he thought it was just a nice slogan to get votes." Who do you think you're kidding, Michelle? That is exactly why he used it.

"He and I and so many," Mrs. Obama continued, "believe that—what else do you have if you don't have hope? What do you give your kids if you can't give them hope?" She is clearly suggesting that only the Obamas' definition of hope is correct, thereby invalidating the hopes and aspirations of the millions who voted for Trump. In reality, Mrs. Obama is nothing more than a sore loser. If you don't believe in what we want you to believe, she is saying, you are an enemy of

A CULTURE OF LIES

hope. Wow! That is monumental leftist arrogance and, frankly, it offends me.

Yes, Barack Obama got away with it for eight years, but at last his hope-a-dope strategy has been unmasked. Now we know what Obama intended by his version of hope and change. The change he tried to induce was the destruction of American exceptionalism by reducing her influence on the world stage and by bringing her down economically and militarily. Obama hoped that the United States would become Denmark. An unexceptional nation, divided from within, and weighed down by the insatiable demands of a massive nanny state. No thank you, Mr. Obama. Please take your hope-a-dope somewhere else, anywhere else, but not here.

In the grand scheme of things, hope-a-dope is not unusual. The Left nurtures a culture of lies in order to further its agenda. At the root of the culture is the corrupt mainstream media. "The media," said Mark Levin, "is a tool of the Left."

In a moment of classic leftist hypocrisy, liberal commentator Ted Koppel told conservative spokesman Sean Hannity that all conservative commentators are bad for this country because they appeal to people who are more interested in ideology than facts. The opposite is true. The left-leaning mainstream media—the *New York Times*, *Washington Post*, CBS, NBC, ABC, MSNBC, and their pals—have surrendered the mantle of objective news reporting. They believe that the purpose of the media is to impose its leftist ideology on the public.

When you read an article on the front page of the *Times*, there is a better-than-even chance that you are reading fact mixed with opinion. Bernard Goldberg has referred to this as "passing off editorial opinion as straight news," where news is distorted in order to influence public opinion. In the halcyon days of journalists such as Edward R. Murrow, Chet

Huntley, David Brinkley, and Eric Sevareid, you could believe what they told you. Not anymore. "The American mainstream media is filled to the brim with liars, frauds, partisans, cheats, plagiarists," claims *Breitbart News Network*, "and those who tolerate, defend and enable all of them."

These are some of the techniques used by the media to fool us:

- Outright falsification of facts.
- Misrepresentation of facts.
- Exaggeration and distortion.
- Downplaying what they don't want you to know.
- Vague source attribution.
- Pejorative labels.
- Omission of facts.
- Selective reporting, or "cherry picking."

The lies of the left-wing media make it difficult for the average citizen to formulate an intelligent opinion on major issues. The Left does not want people to know the truth. Otherwise Democrats would leave the party like rats escaping a sinking ship. Getting to the truth is all but impossible because the mainstream media lies to protect the Left. When they lie, they don't bother to give an explanation. They simply rely on groupthink and the gullibility of the public.

The Media's Favorite Target

Many Americans have a negative opinion of Donald Trump. And that's not because Trump deserves a negative review. It is strictly thanks to our corrupt media. The media sought to torpedo Trump before the election but they failed.

A CULTURE OF LIES

Ignoring the opportunity to modify their slant in favor of objective reporting, they are instead ramping up the volume of malicious lies. "According to recent polls," says the *New York Times*, "the image of Donald Trump as a bigot has begun to crystallize, and for good reason: Because it's true!" A columnist writing in the *Washington Post* says, "Let's not mince words: Donald Trump is a bigot and a racist." Anything but subtle. For those who still read this kind of yellow journalistic garbage, coming away with a positive view of President Trump is all but impossible.

The media also give inordinate space to the ravings of senile Democrats. They loved to quote former Sen. Harry Reid: Trump is a "sexual predator" who has "emboldened the forces of hate and bigotry in America," said Reid. "Winning the electoral college does not absolve Trump of the grave sins he committed against millions of Americans," Reid argued. Trump must "roll back the tide of hate he unleashed."

Let's not forget to include the avid reporting of good old Bernie Sanders' ignorant rant: "To the extent that [Trump] pursues racist, sexist, xenophobic and anti-environment policies," said Sanders, "we will vigorously oppose him." Smoke some more grass, Bernie.

Now let's set the record straight: *None of this spiteful reporting is true.* You can make an argument—albeit a misleading one—that many bigots have supported Trump. That does not make him a racist. As confirmed by Rep. Mo Brooks of Alabama, the Democratic Party's strategy is to divide Americans based on skin pigmentation and to solicit the votes of everybody who is non-white using the argument that whites are discriminatory. This is classic leftist strategy, right out of *Rules for Radicals*. "The Left views blacks as useful idiots in their quest to transform America into a Socialist nation," says African-American entertainer and political activist Lloyd Marcus. Democrats spend half their lives accusing Republicans of not being "for the people," of being racist, sexist, and all the other ists. And for the most part, Republicans let them get away with it. Trump does not.

That's why media attacks on Trump have reached a mad crescendo. Trump's effort to defend himself from unfair and untrue media assaults aggravates the daylights out of the media. For example, according to NBC, not informing the media pool that he was going to dinner shows that Trump is guilty of a "lack of transparency." Commenting on the absurdity of this argument, Sean Hannity facetiously suggested that the media ought to be informed when Trump goes to the toilet and whether it is number one or number two, so they will know how long he will take. But here is the best one: Trump's decision to forgo his presidential salary is alleged to be in violation of the Constitution. Although it was okay for Herbert Hoover and John F. Kennedy, this decision, says *The Atlantic*, suggests that Trump "holds himself above the ordinary rules." With our biased media, you just can't win if your name is Donald Trump.

Since he arrived on the political scene, Trump's opinions on a variety of issues were repudiated at first by the media only to be vindicated as facts came to light. An example is Trump's insistence that the election polls were biased and inaccurate. After relentless attacks by the media, it turned out that he was right after all. Does this matter to the Left? Not one iota. Calling Trump a liar is part of a concerted effort by the Democratic Party and its media allies to undermine his presidency.

Fortunately, two developments are slowing down the attacks. First, the public is becoming more sophisticated in recognizing that the big liar in the room is actually the media itself. After all the falsehoods circulated during the election, the media has a lot of catching up to do if they want to reclaim their reputation for telling the truth. The second development is that we have a president who is no shrinking violet. Unlike George W. Bush, who allowed the media to portray him as a boob, we can count on Trump to defend himself with vigor.

Lies About Israel

Former Secretary of State John Kerry commented on Israel's rejection of a two-state UN resolution condemning Israeli settlements in "occupied territory." Listening to Kerry's statement, I had to shake my head in disbelief. The US Secretary of State argued that you can't be Jewish and democratic. The two are mutually exclusive. I still don't believe he said it.

If Donald Trump had issued a similar statement, the liberal press would have stapled the anti-Semite charge all over his backside. But Trump didn't say it. Kerry did. Where was the outrage from the mainstream media? The *New York Times* reacted as though it never happened. "It is unclear," said the *Times*, "what Mr. Kerry hopes to achieve from the speech." Unclear? Are they joking? Bear in mind that Kerry's speech came only three weeks before Trump was to take over. It sure was a classy way to promote a peaceful transition to the new administration.

Exposing the truth, Israeli Prime Minister Benjamin Netanyahu said Kerry's speech "barely touched upon the root of the conflict—Palestinian opposition to a Jewish state in any boundaries." The Palestinians, along with their Islamic allies in Iran, Saudi Arabia, etc., want nothing less than the destruction of Israel. They are not interested in peace. Their goal is extermination. What Kerry and his boss Obama were advocating is a Palestinian terrorist state right next to Israel. Anything less, said Kerry, would be undemocratic. Are we supposed to take this seriously?

The implication of Kerry's speech is that an Islamic country can deny human rights and at the same time be democratic. No problem there. "Kerry did not mention that Jordan was never subjected to international pressure to grant the Palestinians their own state during the 19 years that Jordan occupied Judea, Samaria, and East Jerusalem," wrote Andrew McCarthy in the *National Review*. That kind of pressure is reserved for Israel. The bottom line, said McCarthy, is that Kerry and Obama refused to acknowledge that the Palestinians "would long ago have had their own state if they had recognized Israel's right to exist and abandoned jihadist terror."

Adding insult to injury, Kerry alleged that, "No American administration has done more for Israel's security than Barack Obama's." This is an outright lie. "From lifting sanctions on Iran to calling for Israel to return to its indefensible 1967 borders," said the *Washington Times*, "Mr. Obama has spent the past seven years betraying America's treasured friend."

Why is Israel always singled out for criticism? Why didn't Kerry acknowledge that Muslim countries are the biggest abusers of human rights on the planet? One answer is that Barack Obama's sympathies—and those of the UN—were aligned with Muslim interests. As former CIA officer and political strategist Clare Lopez has pointed out, Obama's policies with respect to the Islamic world favored our enemies and undermined our allies. It is therefore reasonable to ask the question: Whose side was he on?

Another plausible answer is that picking on the little guy is so much easier. Israel's offense is that it is small. If the population of Israel was the same as Egypt's—80 million—it would be more difficult to slander. If Israel was surrounded by a dozen Jewish states, the UN would be drafting a very different sort of resolution. Unfortunately, the UN has become a toy of the Muslim world—and so was the US government under Obama.

Lies About Climate

It drives me nuts when somebody tries to pull the wool over my eyes. I hate being conned. That's why I am so disturbed by all the manufactured, left-inspired hysteria about climate change. The truth is clearly stated in my book, *In Lies We Trust*:

> "It cannot be claimed beyond a reasonable doubt that (a) global warming exists, or that (b) climate change is caused by human activities, or that (c) climate change is dangerous. I would like to remain open-minded on this issue but the more research I do, the more convinced I am that global warming is a giant hoax."

It used to be suicide to admit that you deny global warming. But now the media, which has supported the GW agenda lock, stock, and barrel, is reacting to an unexpected development: The new president and his EPA administrator are skeptical about climate change. It is finally acceptable to defy Al Gore and his gang of GW bullies. Articles agreeing with my position have been popping up all over the place.

"The oft-repeated claim that nearly all scientists demand that something dramatic be done to stop global warming is not true," a group of distinguished scientists revealed in the *Wall Street Journal*. "In fact, a large and growing number of distinguished scientists and engineers do not agree that drastic actions on global warming are needed." In support of this conclusion is the Global Warming Petition Project, in which 31,000 physicists and physical chemists contend that "there is no convincing scientific evidence that human release of carbon dioxide, methane, or other greenhouse gases is causing or will, in the foreseeable future, cause catastrophic heating of the Earth's atmosphere and disruption of the Earth's climate."

John Coleman, founder of the *Weather Channel*, is one of many skeptics who contradict the validity of GW science. "There is no significant man-made global warming at this time," says Coleman, "there has been none in the past and there is no reason to fear any in the future." But what about all the hysteria over carbon dioxide emissions? "Efforts to prove the theory that carbon dioxide is a significant greenhouse gas and pollutant causing significant warming or weather effects have failed," says Coleman.

Climate change is a natural phenomenon. "Climates and sea levels have always changed," says geologist Ian Plimer, author of *Heaven and Earth: Global Warming, the Missing Science*. "It has been going on for millions of years." Temperature has been constant for 20 years, says Nobel laureate Ivar Giaever, with no unusual rise in sea level. "Climate changes all the time," he says, "and it's nothing to do with global warming."

So why did the Obama Administration try so hard to shove this nonsense down our throats? The answer is that alarmism over climate was used to justify Obama's appetite for bigger government. "The government scares people into thinking that the end is nigh," *The Federalist Papers Project* explained, "and that the only way to turn it around is to cede control to the federal government and allow them to force their economy-killing policies on business."

Climate hysteria also reinforced Obama's globalist aspirations. "One has to free oneself from the illusion that international climate policy is environmental policy," confessed German economist and UN official Ottmar Edenhofer. "Climate policy has almost nothing to do anymore with environmental protection. The next world climate summit is actually an economy summit during which the distribution of the world's resources will be negotiated." Christiana Figueres, executive secretary of the UN's Framework Convention on Climate Change and the driving force behind the 2015 Paris Agreement, admitted that the goal of environmental activists is not to save the world from ecological calamity but to *destroy capitalism*. As reported in *Investor's Business Daily*, Figueres said, "This is the first time in the history of mankind that we are setting ourselves the task of intentionally, within a defined period of time, to change the economic development model that has been reigning for at least 150 years, since the Industrial Revolution."

Climate Change Business Journal quantified the cost of proposed anti-GW measures at a whopping $1.5 trillion per year. That's $1.5 trillion to solve a non-existent problem. An expenditure of that magnitude would destroy the US economy. How do we justify crippling the US economy in pursuit of ghosts—what do we get for this waste of time, money, and effort? Danish environmentalist Bjorn Lomborg calculates that even if every nation in the world adheres to its climate change commitments by 2030, by the end of this century it will reduce the world's temperatures by a mere 0.048°C or 1/20th of a degree Celsius. Is this not a monumental hoax? Mark Levin sums it up in *Plunder and Deceit*:

> "*The politicization and radicalization of the environmental movement into a primitive, degrowth, anticapitalism movement built on a foundation of junk science and emotionalism...directly threatens two centuries of human progress and the unparalleled American lifestyle. Its campaign to undo the*

Industrial Revolution and blunt the modern technological revolution will result in economic contraction while further empowering the federal government's grip on daily human activity. The so-called Green Movement is, in fact, an anti-liberty and antiopportunity movement aimed at changing the nation in ways that will deprive younger people and future generations of their full potential."

In other words, we are being duped by groupthink on climate. This is precisely what Al Gore tried to do. In his phony 2006 film, *An Inconvenient Truth*, Gore made a series of ridiculous predictions. He claimed that, due to global warming, melting ice would cause a 20-foot rise in sea level "in the near future." Then he predicted that the Arctic summer ice would "completely disappear" within five years. His most frightening prediction, guaranteed to give nightmares to children, was that the world had until January 2016 to end its addiction to fossil fuels or it would *come to an end*. It's lucky for us that he was a lame prophet. Ben Shapiro nailed it when he observed that the environmental movement creates a crisis and then lies about it, falsifying evidence to convince people to give up their standard of living or we will all die. Mommy!

A Vote of No Confidence

The media have been reporting on so many scandals and pseudo-scandals that it is difficult to navigate through the fog. First there was the "Russians tried to influence the election" scandal, then they added "The Obama administration illegally surveilled the Trump election campaign" scandal, then we have "The deep state composed of Obama supporters is trying to take down Trump" scandal, and now we have the "Who leaked classified information all over the place?" scandal. There is no evidence for the first, and a lot of possibilities with the others. Getting to the bottom of it all will require thorough investigation.

Here is where the real scandal is taking place: We were unable to rely on anyone in the outgoing government to conduct a competent, unbiased investigation. Under Obama, the Justice Department, the FBI, and the IRS were compromised by partisanship the likes of which we have not seen since the Nixon administration. Yet no one was indicted, let alone convicted: Hillary Clinton in connection with Benghazi, selling influence via the Clinton Foundation, and her gross negligence with the emails; Lois Lerner for using the IRS to target conservatives; Black Panthers for interfering with the election process; Loretta Lynch for conspiring with Bill Clinton; Susan Rice for lying to Congress; Obama himself for ignoring the Constitution. Where was justice when we needed it?

The bottom fell out with former FBI Director James Comey's detailed enumeration of Hillary Clinton's transgressions followed by his unwillingness to recommend indictment. People on both sides of the political spectrum were shocked. How could we not attribute his decision to partisanship? Was he bought off? The FBI director is a cop, says former US Attorney Joe DiGenova, not a prosecutor. Comey, he says, usurped the function of the Justice Department. Justice should have made the decision of whether or not to prosecute Clinton. Instead, Comey made the decision and was never held accountable in large part because the Attorney General was compromised by her unexplained meeting with Bill Clinton, the husband of the person under investigation. What a sewer.

Today we have members of Congress expressing their opinions on the various scandals but no action. The public has lost confidence in the government's ability to monitor itself. That is the scandal: Loss of confidence in our government. According to *Pew Research Center*, only 19% of Americans say they can trust the government "always" or "most of the time," among the lowest levels in the past half-century. The NBC/Wall Street Journal poll gives Congress 16% approval and the federal government 22%. The Gallup poll said only 9% of respondents report "a great deal" or "quite a lot" of confidence in Congress. "Congress keeps getting worse," says MSNBC, "and its support keeps reaching new depths, but the prospects for change appear remote, at best."

Congressional oversight, derived from the "implied powers" in the Constitution, is designed to monitor governmental activities via the congressional committee system. Many reports since 9/11 have criticized congressional oversight of the intelligence community. "There is no accountability," said Sen. Chuck Hagel. "Oversight of the intelligence community is a joke." The reason, said the late columnist Nat Hentoff, is the "culture of revolving-door cronyism." As far back as 1978, Watergate prosecutor Leon Jaworski recommended that prominent citizens with no governmental ties be appointed to investigate branches of government.

Another problem is that House and Senate Intelligence Committees lack the technical skills necessary for a hacking investigation. "Committee staff are underwater when it comes to poking into the nitty gritty of cyber warfare," says *The Intercept*, "a longstanding problem made more relevant as attacks on US government and politicians escalate."

The FBI has conducted a nearly year long investigation into the so-called Russian scandal—which so far has yielded no proof—but they are reluctant to investigate the myriad of leaks of top-secret information and the unlawful surveillance of private citizens. Rep. Devin Nunes, chairman of the House Intelligence Committee, has accused the FBI of refusing to cooperate with House investigations of NSA surveillance of the Trump campaign.

I am living in hope that the Sessions Justice Department will change the ball game, although it concerns me that Sessions has recused himself from the Russian hacking issue. The Justice Department's inspector general has announced that the FBI is investigating Comey's public statements as well as FBI leaks and other relevant correspondences. Perhaps we will eventually get to the bottom of things, but for now it appears unlikely. That would suit the Left to a tee.

Chapter Ten
Black Hair and Campus Brainwashing

"Black Hair as Culture and History" is an upper-level history seminar that has been offered at prestigious Stanford University, known as the Harvard of the Pacific and often ranked as the number one university in the country. It concerns how black hair "has interacted with the black presence in this country, and how it has played a role in the evolution of black society." The course syllabus includes: "Early Black Hair in America," "The Birth of Straightened Hair," "New Ideas on Black Hair," "The Rise of the Afro," and "The Economic and Status Importance of Black Hair." The seminar concludes with "The Great Debate": Should blacks straighten their hair or remain natural? (I'm not making this up. Honest.) Such useless classes are mandated for graduation at Stanford. This and a raft of other wacko courses have replaced traditional ones such as Western Civilization and Great Literature. After all, who gives a damn about Plato, Shakespeare, and Freud?

This information was obtained from *The Diversity Myth* by David Sacks and Peter Thiel—both of whom are Stanford graduates. I have no reason to doubt their veracity, but I can't help thinking that it is too ridiculous to be true. Sacks and Thiel have this to say about "Black Hair":

> "The absurd race consciousness of "Black Hair" is a testament to the extremes to which multiculturalism has taken the curriculum. The new thinking and new disciplines that loftily promised to 'broaden horizons' and 'open minds' in reality teach students banalities. Rather than helping students to surmount superficial racial differences, the new curriculum has enshrined them in an attempt to make minority students feel good... Moreover, they have revamped much of the more mainstream curriculum to incorporate elements found in "Black Hair"—the class's therapeutic function, its adulation of trendiness, its emphasis on victims and victimhood, and its radicalizing of differences."

Twenty years ago, I would not have believed that our institutions of higher learning have turned into "left-wing madhouses." The entire campus situation today is beyond belief. If I was shelling out $100,000 per year to send my kid to some fancy college only to discover that they are teaching courses like this one, I would pull my kid out of there faster than you can say "New Ideas on Black Hair." But maybe I'm just an old fart.

I was not always conservative in my thinking. My family were liberal Democrats. So were most of the people in my Brooklyn neighborhood. As I passed through adolescence and young adulthood, I met many liberals who resembled Bernie Sanders. These arrogant taskmasters acted as though they had obtained special permission to tell me how I ought to think. Some of them were professors at the college I attended. In spite of them, or perhaps because of them, I came to believe in two things: evidence and common sense. I observed that whatever the issue, the liberal view usually is devoid of evidence, lacking in common sense, and full of hypocrisy. That was when I became a conservative. I can thank Brooklyn College for giving me a tremendous advantage in life by teaching me how to think for myself.

Today's college student is being taught a different set of priorities. American colleges and universities don't care about teaching their students how to think. Former Yale University President Benno Schmidt said, "The assumption seems to be that the purpose of education is to induce correct opinion rather than to search for wisdom and to liberate the mind." Our educational system has become an incubator for the Left. All they want to do is brainwash the kids to parrot the Left's dogmatic ideology. I am appalled not only by what is happening on campuses today but by what it portends for the future. "Give me four years to teach the children," said Lenin, "and the seed I have sown will never be uprooted."

Tyranny of the Majority

A friend of mine who is a professor at a well-known college confessed to me that he has to keep his mouth shut because so few of his colleagues share his conservative outlook. This time we are dealing with the tyranny of the majority. A study by the UCLA Higher Education Research Institute found that 62.7% of full-time faculty at four-year colleges and universities identify as liberal or far left. Only 11.9% identify as conservative or far right. Another poll pegged liberals at 87% and conservatives at 13%. In some schools, says Walter E. Williams, professor of economics at George Mason University, the ratio of Democrats to Republicans can be as high as 20-1. A recent study identified

Democrats to Republicans in journalism departments of 1,500 universities at 20-1, and a whopping 33.5-1 in history departments. "The next time you hear a college president boasting about how diverse his college is," Williams suggests, "ask him how many Republican faculty members there are in his journalism, psychology, English, and sociology departments." Thomas Sowell says:

> "The real money, for intellectuals at least, is overwhelmingly on the left. Black intellectuals, especially, can easily earn six-figure incomes just from lecture fees alone at colleges and universities around the country. All it takes are some heated accusations of 'racism' against whites and denunciations of American society in general, with perhaps a few anti-semitic remarks thrown in for good measure."

The question is, when did this happen? How did campuses become fueling stations for the Left? According to Ben Shapiro in *Bullies*, college administrators decided in the 1960s that it was "easier to appease rampaging leftist students than to deal with them. They came to an agreement with the wildebeests: stop taking over the buildings and locking the doors, and we'll start teaching you about how America sucks." Gradually that translated into liberalism becoming a prerequisite for getting hired. Many campuses require new faculty members to sign a "diversity statement." They are forced to pledge allegiance to the college's leftist agenda, says Professor Williams. "What diversity oaths seek," he says, "is to maintain political conformity among the faculty indoctrinating our impressionable, intellectually immature young people."

For example, UC San Diego requires a "Contributions to Diversity Statement" that describes one's experience, activities and future plans to advance diversity, equity, and inclusion. Diversity in this case means racial, sex, and sexual orientation quotas. "Colleges spend billions of dollars on offices of diversity and inclusion, diversity classes, and diversity indoctrination," says Professor Williams. "The last thing that diversity hustlers want is diversity in ideas."

The Big Bashers

Two destructive leftist agendas have taken over on campus. One has to do with bashing whites and the other with bashing all things American. Both are presented as part of the push for multiculturalism and victimhood.

"The momentum of the present is veering toward tribalism, not unity," says Scott Greer in *No Campus for White Men*. "And the only thing keeping all the tribes of the Left unified right now is their shared animosity toward whites." The campus of today is a victimhood culture where whites are morally inferior and blacks are superior because of their presumed history of oppression.

The kind of diversity championed by college administrators is about group conflict. From African-American activists demanding racial quotas to transsexuals urging the elimination of gender-specific pronouns, Greer observes, "a protected class is nearly always at the center of a college outrage."

"The one group not allowed to have a powerful identity is whites," says Greer, who explains the campus situation in terms of identity politics that encourage minority students to demand power solely based on race, gender, or sexual orientation. It's a species of identity politics, he says, "that's increasingly bordering on outright hatred for white people, especially white men." Skin color matters more than shared political principles. The identity of the person behind the ideas is more important than the ideas themselves. A white person who agrees with the leftist agenda will still be marginalized because of his skin color.

The Left—a vocal and powerful minority of students—wants to portray America as "an incurable mass of bigoted whites," says Ben Shapiro. They want whites to "bend over backwards to make amends." But no matter what they do, says Shapiro, whites will "never be done paying the piper."

One of the most popular forms of anti-white discrimination is the indoctrination training forced by many colleges on white freshmen. The purpose, says Greer, is to make whites feel badly about their skin color. Whites should "sit down, shut up, and allow their moral superiors to berate them." Actually, they are already indoctrinated by the time they arrive in college. The *New York Post* exposed the Bank Street School, an elite private school in Manhattan, where they are teaching white students as young as six that "they're born racist and should feel guilty about benefiting from 'white privilege,'" while their black peers are "taught to feel proud about their race and are rewarded with treats and other privileges." White parents have complained about how their children are indoctrinated into thinking that systemic racism still exists, that they are part of the problem, and that "any success they achieve is unearned." Parents are upset that the school "deliberately instills in white children a strong sense of guilt about their race." A six-year-old came home in tears, saying, "I'm a bad person." This is nothing short of disgusting.

A new college course offering is "Whiteness Studies," designed to force white students to rub their own noses in their allegedly ingrained racism and white privilege. David Horowitz made the wry observation that black studies celebrates blackness, Chicano studies celebrates Chicanos, and whiteness studies "attacks white people as evil." It is amazing that schools are getting away with this.

Taking it even one step further is Tommy Curry, an African-American professor at Texas A&M. In his course on "Radical Black Philosophies," Curry advocates "Critical Race Theory" where he says that black people should talk openly about murdering white people. The murder of white people, Curry says, may be necessary to achieve black liberation. He wants white people to fear blacks so much that they believe "death could come for them at any moment."

In Chapter Three, I explained how the Left's payoff from its diversity and multicultural agenda is stoking racial discord. In our colleges and universities, multiculturalism actually creates racial division where none existed previously. At Stanford, for example, they discovered that most minority students share backgrounds that are similar to white students. The question that occurred to Sacks and Thiel is: "Why does orientation exaggerate differences that were almost nonexistent upon students' arrival at Stanford?" The answer: Minorities are forced to be "different" only after they have been separated by the Stanford administration. It is done deliberately to justify the multicultural mythology that has taken over the school.

Segregation, say Sacks and Thiel, still exists on college campuses. In the name of multiculturalism, universities like Cornell, Berkeley, and Stanford segregate different ethnic groups in "race dormitories." The net result of this "ghettoizing" is to remove a large number of minority students from the rest of the campus and to limit diversity of interaction. Stanford, Vanderbilt, University of Michigan, Berkeley and other schools conduct separate graduation ceremonies for different minority groups, "further dividing the campus along racial lines."

"The primary problem for multiculturalists," say Sacks and Thiel, "is that there are almost no real racists at Stanford or, for that matter, in America's younger generation." In other words, the whole thing is a farce manufactured by the Left in order to foment discontent.

The same conclusion applies to incidents of racism on campus. Most college-age students are tolerant and open-minded. When minority students at Stanford were asked to describe concrete examples of campus racism, few were able to do so and many were bewildered by the suggestion that racism is prevalent. In order for Stanford to maintain the fiction of clear-cut racial identities, it has been necessary to manufacture evidence of cradle-to-grave oppression. Without the counterfeit evidence, the entire multicultural farce implodes.

Related to the anti-white movement on campus is the proliferation of anti-American propaganda. "College campuses have become fascist colonies of anti-American hate speech," says Ann Coulter. "Presenting terrorists in a sympathetic light and the US as an imperialist nation is standard fare," reports Ashley Edwardson on Allen B. West's website. "This is what, in varying degrees, most college kids are learning today, all over the country. What's even worse is that students apparently are not free to defend our country, express different points of view, or even disagree with the class instructor."

The students at UC Irvine voted to remove all American flags from "inclusive spaces" on campus because of their "offensive" nature. A professor at Metropolitan State University of Denver requires his students to recite an anti-American pledge of allegiance. Political scientist Alan Wolfe, after surveying major texts used in American Studies courses, said that, "Scholars in the field have developed a hatred for America so visceral that it makes one wonder why they bother studying America at all."

Three infamous collegiate America bashers are Ward

Churchill, Nicholas de Genova, and Noam Chomsky. Churchill (Colorado University) tried to justify terrorist activity against the US as a rightful response to American aggression. De Genova (Columbia) advocated the killing of American soldiers in Somalia. MIT Professor Noam Chomsky has stated that 9/11 was a justifiable retaliation against American injustice. With teachers like these, is it any wonder that our campuses are a hotbed of anti-American radicalism?

It is worthy of mention that the left-wing anti-American agenda that exists on American campuses has a stalwart supporter in George Soros. Through his Open Society Foundations, Soros is believed to have contributed more than $400 million to advance his radical ideology at colleges and universities. Soros is a billionaire who believes in income redistribution, socialism, globalism, global warming, and all things anti-American. He has contributed untold millions to support Barack Obama, Hillary Clinton, ACORN, La Raza, Southern Poverty Law Center, Huffington Post, Media Matters, MoveOn.org, Center for American Progress, and other leftist organizations. The word on the street is that Soros is behind the violent anti-Trump protests. He has remained a somewhat enigmatic figure. "I admit that I have always harbored an exaggerated view of my self-importance," Soros said. "To put it bluntly, I fancied myself as some kind of god." As in the case of Obama, it is to be hoped that the public eventually will learn the truth about what kind of god Soros really is.

Assault on Free Speech

Intellectual freedom on campus is flirting with extinction. Students in the 1960s demanded more freedom, says Greer, particularly freedom of speech. Today's students demand less freedom and actually want to limit free expression.

According to a 2014 study, close to 60% of the 400-plus colleges surveyed "seriously infringe upon the free speech rights of students." *And the students are for it.* Political correctness on campus is giving rise to a new generation that is poised to throw free speech out the window.

Activists believe free speech is their exclusive province. Contrary opinions are oppressive and labeled as hate speech. "Campus leftists," says Greer, "are able to suppress all dissenting speech for the supposed good of humanity."

In a poll of 800 undergraduates conducted by McLaughlin & Associates, 51% of students—yes, a majority—favored codes on campus limiting free speech. 30% of students who identified as "liberal" said *the First Amendment is outdated.* 72% of students agreed that, "Any student or faculty member on campus who uses language that is considered racist, sexist, homophobic or otherwise offensive should be subject to disciplinary action." The Higher Education Research Institute at UCLA surveyed 141,189 college students. 71% agreed with the statement that, "Colleges should prohibit racist/sexist speech on campus."

Political commentator Kirsten Powers writes in *The Daily Beast* that our colleges have "invented a labyrinth of anti-free speech tools that include 'speech codes,' 'free speech zones,' censorship, investigations by campus 'diversity and tolerance offices,' and denial of due process. They craft 'anti-harassment policies' and 'anti-violence policies' that are speech codes in disguise." Powers explains that, "Speech codes are weapons to silence anyone—professors, students, visiting speakers—who expresses a view that deviates from the left's worldview or ideology."

Many campus speech codes are obviously racist. At Stanford, the speech code was written to prohibit "fighting words" directed at other students. It outlawed words intended to insult students based on their race, sex, color, sexual orientation, religion, ethnic origin, handicap, etc. The catch, however, was that only members of "subordinated" groups (i.e., minority victims) could be insulted. Once again, whites (considered oppressors, not victims) were left without any protection from the allegedly hostile environment.

"The belief that free speech rights don't include the right to speak offensively is now firmly entrenched on campuses and enforced by repressive speech or harassment codes," writes attorney and author Wendy Kaminer in *The Atlantic*. Campus censors, she says, "insist that hate speech isn't free speech and that people who indulge in it should be punished."

Here is an oft-quoted example: An editorial at Wellesley College insisted that the right to free expression is not guaranteed by the Constitution. "Shutting down rhetoric that undermines the existence and rights of others is not a violation of free speech; it is hate speech. The founding fathers put free speech in the Constitution as a way to protect the disenfranchised... The spirit of free speech is to protect the suppressed, not to protect a free-for-all where anything is acceptable, no matter how hateful and damaging." This self-serving definition of free speech clearly is a distortion of the First Amendment as interpreted by the courts.

And here is the kicker: When these campus censors refer to *hate speech*, they mean anything that they disagree with. So it is free speech for them but the hell with everybody else. George Orwell warned about this problem in *Nineteen Eighty-Four*. We saw it come to fruition in Nazi Germany. Now it is our problem.

William Deresiewicz, author of *Excellent Sheep*, writes in *The American Scholar* that the first thing many students learn when they get to college is to keep quiet about political views, Christian faith, non-feminist views about marriage, and just about anything else. How come? Because they never know when they might say something that they're not supposed to. He cites the example of students who were told they couldn't use the expression "that's a crazy idea" because it would stigmatize the mentally ill. A young woman was criticized by a fellow student for wearing moccasins—an act, she was informed, of *cultural appropriation*. Above all, Deresiewicz says, his students tell him that political correctness has simply gone too far—way too far. Everybody feels oppressed, as they put it, by the "PC police."

Behind the attack on free speech is the acceptance of "emotional reasoning," where feelings determine the interpretation of reality. If someone is upset, that proves something is wrong. Emotional reasoning has given birth to a slew of new concepts: free speech zones, safe spaces, trigger warnings, and hostile environments.

Free speech zones are defined areas on campus where students must go if they want to express unpopular ideas. *Safe spaces*, which usually include most of the campus, are places that discourage free expression. They prohibit words and ideas that are likely to make some students (i.e., minorities) uncomfortable. Claims of a right not to be offended have become commonplace, and universities have continued to enable them. The argument is that most college students are overgrown children in need of protection from *hostile environments.*

What constitutes a hostile environment? When Republicans at Emory University chalked "Trump 2016" on the sidewalks, liberal students called it racial intimidation and asked school administrators to condemn it. University officials defended the protestors on the grounds that students from marginalized groups experience unimaginable levels of intolerance and they have a right to demand a campus free from offense. Indiana University found a white student guilty of racial harassment for reading a book entitled *Notre Dame vs. the Klan*. Although the book honored student opposition to the Ku Klux Klan when it marched on Notre Dame in 1924, the picture of a Klan rally on the book's cover offended at least one student. That was enough for a guilty finding by the university's Affirmative Action Office.

In 2013, the Departments of Justice and Education broadened the definition of sexual harassment to include verbal conduct that is simply "unwelcome." Greg Lukianoff and Jonathan Haidt, authors of "The Coddling of the American Mind" in *The Atlantic*, explain what this means:

> "Out of fear of federal investigations, universities are now applying that standard—defining unwelcome speech as harassment—not just to sex, but to race, religion, and veteran status as well. Everyone is supposed to rely upon his or her own subjective feelings to decide whether a comment by a professor or a fellow student is unwelcome, and therefore grounds for a harassment claim. Emotional reasoning is now accepted as evidence."

My problem with safe spaces is that they serve as another way to control speech on campus, and they place students in a cocoon that prevents them from being exposed to new ideas. "If they want to be safe from ideas," said Alan Dershowitz, "there are better places to be than colleges and university campuses."

Another device for protecting fragile students is the *trigger warning*, alerting the student that what he is reading or viewing contains potentially disturbing material. Lukianoff and Haidt offer the observation that trigger warnings and safe spaces teach students to think "pathologically," which can lead to mental illness. They also fail to prepare students for professional life, which often demands intellectual engagement with people and ideas one might find offensive or disturbing. It will be interesting to see what these snowflakes do when they are confronted with the harsh reality of daily existence.

Campus censorship is not limited to public speech. Private conversations are not safe either, as two students at Lewis & Clark College discovered when someone turned them in for allegedly making racially offensive comments at a private party. Gender pronouns (he, she) also have come under attack. Some administrations back the use of "gender-neutral" pronouns to avoid offending transgender students. Under threat of coercion, they want to compel the use of language that Jordan Peterson describes as "not common or even useful."

Finally, I want to expose the intolerance encountered by conservatives who have attempted to speak at college campuses. David Horowitz has described his constant harassment by leftist students, an experience that has been shared by Harvard Professor Alan Dershowitz. Others, such as former Secretary of State Condoleezza Rice, Christine Lagarde, managing director of the International Monetary Fund, and former Muslim Ayaan Hirsi Ali, have been turned away by student and faculty objections.

Conservative speakers on campus have to wear bulletproof vests and audience members are regularly assaulted by hordes of black-clad protestors. Author Heather Mac Donald was overwhelmed by mob violence when she attempted to speak at Claremont McKenna College in California. This is an excerpt from a letter to the college written by a group of black students:

"If engaged, Heather Mac Donald would not be debating on mere difference of opinion, but the right of Black people to exist. Heather Mac Donald is a fascist, a white supremacist, a warhawk, a transphobe, a queerphobe, a classist, and ignorant of interlocking systems of domination that produce the lethal conditions under which oppressed peoples are forced to live... Advocating for white supremacy and giving white supremacists platforms wherefrom their toxic and deadly illogic may be disseminated is condoning violence against Black people."

All the allegations in the letter are false. "I felt like I was in the French Revolution," Mac Donald said. "It was as if they were coming to take me to the guillotine." This is an apt metaphor for campus madness, which often bears a resemblance to the reigns of terror that occurred during the revolutions in France, Russia, China, and elsewhere. Who could have guessed it would happen here?

The Shape of Things to Come

David Horowitz urges Republicans to force universities to add "intellectual and political diversity" into their mission statements. This might force them to hire conservative professors for a long overdue change.

Lukianoff and Haidt recommend that Congress should define harassment based on the Supreme Court's definition in the 1999 case of *Davis v. Monroe County Board of Education*. The *Davis* standard holds that a single comment or thoughtless remark by a student does not equal harassment. Harassment requires a "pattern of objectively offensive behavior" by one student that interferes with another student's access to education. "Establishing the *Davis* standard," say Lukianoff and Haidt, "would help eliminate universities' impulse to police their students' speech so carefully."

Greer projects a disturbing view of the possible social and political discourse in America's future. The kids marching today to shut down a speaker they don't like could very well be the senators, judges, and newspaper editors of tomorrow. A survey has alleged that 53% of millennials have a favorable view of socialism. Gallup found that 69% of millennials say they would vote for a socialist candidate for president. (Did you hear that, Bernie Sanders?) Our country could be run by people who think extreme identity politics is terrific, that all white people are racists, that protected classes should never be offended, and that conservative viewpoints should be prohibited. "And it all could begin," says Greer, "with colleges doling out spoils to those with the highest degree of victim status."

"All of these factors combine to make higher education toxic for serious intellectual development and bode ill for the country's future," says Greer. *"If everyone is vying to be the top victim and the most oppressed by Western civilization, campus life becomes more likely to descend into a veritable war of all against all."*

If white guilt becomes an unchallenged dogma, hate against whites will increase as nonwhites are told to blame their failures in life on white supremacy, and are taught to see Western history as one long tale of oppression. Eventually there will be a white backlash. That is part of the Left's program. A civil war between races and ethnic groups is entirely possible. It is happening now in France between native-born French and Muslim immigrants. It can happen to us.

We can only hope that white students will recover from the campaign to instill white guilt and that non-white students will recognize the benefits of embracing traditional American values. A great deal of responsibility must be placed on white parents who allow their offspring to be the objects of racist abuse. I would like to see these parents pull their kids out of offending colleges or threaten to withhold financial contributions if courses on black hair continue to replace Shakespeare. Hitting the enemy in the pocketbook is always an effective means of fighting back.

Let me leave this chapter with one last thought. When asked why American voters have lost their ability to see through obvious nonsense, Thomas Sowell replied, "That was before nonsense became a large part of the curriculum of our educational institutions."

The Left is licking its chops as America's hallowed educational institutions are being pulled down stone by stone. So much for the shape of things to come. It isn't pretty.

Chapter Eleven
The Great Orange Hope

We began in Chapter One with an examination of Obama's legacy, a quiver of poisoned arrows aimed at the ideological heart of America. Obama's actions while in office formed a tribute to the radical leftists who inspired his attempted takedown of the republic. It is fitting that we end with the antithesis of Obama, a man whose political career was set in motion by his predecessor's contempt for the United States. Radio talk show host Dennis Prager describes Donald Trump:

> "Donald Trump is a conservative dream. From appointing a conservative to the Supreme Court, to approving the Keystone XL pipeline, to weakening the fanatical, hysterical, and tyrannical EPA, to appointing an ambassador to the United Nations who has moral contempt for that immoral institution, to backing Israel, to seeking to reduce economy-choking regulations on business—indeed essentially everything conservatives would wish for in a president—Donald Trump is almost too good to be true."

David Horowitz, in *Big Agenda*, explains Trump's popularity:

> "Donald Trump took up the cause of the forgotten working class, promising to restore America's industrial prowess and bring back the jobs that a corrupt elite with a globalist outlook had negotiated away in reckless trade deals that sent Americans to the back of the bus and squandered the prosperity they had created over generations."

"Trump rejected minority identity politics," says Scott Greer, "failed to acknowledge his 'white privilege,' and ignored the phenomenon of 'systemic racism.'" Ilana Mercer, in *The Trump Revolution*, describes Trump's unique position on the delicate subject of race:

> "No presidential candidate should be in the business of catering to ethnic or racial passions. It's refreshing how switched-off Trump is from the racial grievance industry. Trump is threatening to destabilize the pillars of the Racial-Industrial-Complex. The no-longer-silent majority is exhausted. Americans are exhausted from being racially ramrodded. They've had enough of the pigment burden. The noisy-as-hell-majority is sick-and-tired of being falsely accused of infractions it's innocent of."

David Horowitz agrees:

> "Trump's inclusiveness is all but overlooked by a biased national media, which worked hard to portray him as a bigot, a misogynist, an Islamophobe, a xenophobe, and in general, deplorable."

Throughout the presidential campaign, the Left and their media supporters floated the manufactured assertion that Donald Trump is racist, fascist, and misogynistic. That assertion about Trump is, and always has been, completely false. "The chief strategy of Democratic political campaigns is to use character assassination, otherwise referred to as 'the politics of personal destruction,' as the weapon of choice," says David Horowitz.

"The arguments against Trump do not rely on reasonable assertions of political differences," says Scott Greer, "but on identity concerns. 'Trump makes me feel unsafe as a bisexual Latino' is all that's needed to make the case." But this media strategy, initially designed to destroy Trump's appeal as a candidate, didn't work because the electorate didn't buy it. The same lie was offered up by the Democrats, in conjunction with unsubstantiated claims that the Russians hacked the election, to explain away the failure of Hillary Clinton's candidacy.

The media will not concede that Trump brings to government an unparalleled record of achievement. Instead of focusing on the admirable characteristics of this man who went from political neophyte to incredible victory, NBC refused to relinquish the refuted charge that Trump called Mexicans "rapists" and "killers." Ugly. Untrue. Lies, all of it. But the media onslaught has been overwhelming.

On MSNBC, Rachel Maddow criticized Trump's acceptance speech on the grounds that it was "militant" and "anti-Semitic." Referring to Trump's "America First" slogan, Maddow said it has "very dark echoes in American history." She was alluding to the America First Committee of the 1930s that was infiltrated by Nazis. Terry Moran on ABC agreed that Trump's speech had anti-Semitic "overtones." *Meet the Press* moderator Chuck Todd called the speech "surprisingly divisive." Not to be outdone, Chris Matthews on MSNBC called the speech "Hitlerian!" "If you tell a lie big enough and keep repeating it," said Hitler's propaganda chief Joseph Goebbels, "people will eventually come to believe it."

By aiming to unify the country in its own self-interest, Trump was being described as divisive and Hitlerian. Does the media really believe this nonsense? Comparing Trump's slogan of America First to the isolationist position before World War II is a distortion of history. Trump wants to substitute love of country for Obama's anti-American ideology. How does this make Trump out to be anti-Semitic? Hitlerian? On what planet is there a logical connection? Not this one, to be sure.

If we are going to accuse anyone of anti-Semitism, let's stick with Obama. As Alan Dershowitz has finally figured out, Obama lied to the Jewish community from day one. "From lifting sanctions on Iran to calling for Israel to return to its indefensible 1967 borders," said the *Washington Times*, Obama is guilty of "betraying America's treasured friend." Trump, in stark contrast, has expressed unqualified support for Israel. His daughter and grandchildren are Jewish. Nothing Hitlerian about that.

Nor can we call Trump's intention to place limits on Muslim immigration Hitlerian. Trump has taken serious criticism because he understands the threat posed by Islamic terrorism and the unwillingness of Muslims to accept our values and assimilate into our communities. Obama's failure to mount a serious response to the 28,000 instances of Islamic terrorism since 9/11 was a national disgrace. Hillary was hell bent on perpetuating Obama's head-in-the-sand policy. Let's be thankful that Trump is a realist.

Trump's acceptance speech was the first really positive, forward-looking expression of "American exceptionalism" that we have heard in a long time. He wants to "bind the wounds of division." He wants to give power back to the people. He wants to put an end to self-serving politicians who sell out their constituencies. He wants to put an end to Islamic terror. He wants to find "common ground" and "partnership" with the rest of the world. He wants safer neighborhoods, better schools, good jobs. To call him out as racist, fascist, misogynistic—and let's not forget Hitlerian—is insane.

If the media want to survive, they need to learn the lesson of this election. The mainstream media did everything in their power to elevate Hillary Clinton and destroy Donald Trump. They failed. We have proof that the public is not as gullible as it once was, that the propaganda disseminated by the press is recognized for what it is—not by everyone, but by enough voters and newspaper readers to make a difference.

The irony of the media's strategy is that, although they were in the tank for Hillary, the media were largely responsible for Trump's victory. Does that sound like a self-contradiction? Let me explain.

First, the media gave Trump an extraordinary amount of free airtime. The *New York Times* reported that Trump spent less on TV advertising—the single biggest expenditure for a campaign—than Bush, Rubio, Sanders, Clinton, Cruz, Christie, or Kasich. Bush spent 82 million. Clinton spent 30 million. Trump spent a paltry 10 million, but as of March 15, 2016, *he had received two billion dollars worth of free media attention.* That is more than the total for all the other candidates from both major parties.

"Donald Trump's campaign for president has received more nightly news attention than all the Democratic campaigns combined," reported CNN. "Donald Trump is everywhere," said *The Atlantic*. "The Republican nominee is all anyone can talk about. Whether this is because the media is doing its duty or because news organizations are capitalizing on Trump's bombast for ratings and traffic is a matter of debate." According to *The Tyndall Report*, Trump is "by far the most newsworthy storyline of campaign 2016, accounting for more than a quarter of all coverage" on the evening newscasts of CBS, NBC, and ABC.

The media tried to explain away their outsized coverage of Trump by saying they were largely critical of him. My view is that it doesn't matter if Trump's coverage was positive or negative. I have always believed in the old saw that there is no such thing as bad publicity. Trump's victory proves it. A study from Harvard's *Kennedy School of Government* concluded that, in spite of media anti-Trump bias, most of the Trump media coverage actually was positive *in its impact on voters*. "Trump is arguably the first bona fide media-created presidential nominee," the study alleged. "Although he subsequently tapped a political nerve, journalists fueled his launch."

The second reason to conclude that the media was responsible for Trump's victory is that the obvious anti-Trump media bias drove many undecided voters into his camp. In other words, the media's negativity backfired. "The media's Trump bashing may wind up having the exact opposite of its intended effect," proclaimed a *Los Angeles Times* op-ed piece. "With Trump calling out media organizations for their bias, widespread slanted reporting is bound to reinforce this point—and to backfire." *Executive Intelligence Review* senior editor Jeff Steinberg said, "Media elites thought they were shaping public opinion, and they were, but in favor of Trump because anyone who the mainstream media hates is just fine with them." Writing in *American Thinker*, Karin McQuillan suggested that "the more the media attacks Trump as the second coming of Hitler, the more his supporters become determined to elect him and the more independents join our side."

Agreeing that media bias backfired, one voter wrote, "The bias was so obvious that it created sympathy (and votes) for Trump. People simply rebelled against a 'rigged' (media) system." Another voter said, "I can't sit idly by and allow these perpetrators of fraud to celebrate. Essentially, I am voting for Trump because of the people who don't want me to." Here is the reaction of one disaffected voter to anti-Trump bias on NPR:

"I slammed the radio off after getting so angry at the biased report and decided that moment I am voting for Trump. I had heard the bias before, always kind of subconsciously ignored it. This time I couldn't. I stopped listening to sound bytes from mainstream media, I started listening to full speeches of Trump. When I did that, the most obvious bias became apparent, and today NPR just blew the lid. This media bias is real, it's really intense and it pisses me off."

Media Research Center's president Brent Bozell acknowledged that the media are in "full panic mode" because the American people rejected their leftist agenda—and them.

Sore-loser Democrats are calling Donald Trump a lot of names that include the word "orange." "Big hairy orange villain." "Orange manatee." "Orange Julius." And even the "tangerine tornado." Taking her cue from the media, a woman posted on Facebook that Trump is "a vile, orange, bloated, narcissistic, dangerously thin-skinned, spineless, lying miscreant." I have my own name for him: *The Great Orange Hope.*

The Destabilization Campaign

The most significant thing Trump represents is a pushback by the Right against the destructive ideology of the Left. Prior to Trump, the Right was unwilling to say out loud that leftist policies are treacherous. There is a danger in remaining silent while the Left bloviates. We have to sell American values because they are superior. Not everyone is equal. Not all value systems are equal. But we are all better off if we are faithful to American values.

The Left is not giving up. Says Monica Crowley:

> *"There is a very dangerous and very effective destabilization campaign underway against this president, his administration, and his agenda. The reason they have to destroy him is that Donald Trump is an alien organism that has been injected into the body politic by the American people to reform it. He must not be allowed to succeed."*

The DNC/Clinton/Obama political machine may have lost the election, but they succeeded in whipping up a mindless frenzy among their "deplorable" voting constituency. The big fear in Liberal Land was that Trump would not honor the election results—if he lost. Now that Trump has won, the Left is doing exactly what they claimed Trump would do. Coming out in force with Nazi-style demonstrations. Calling Trump every name in the book. Trump spews hate. He targets minorities. He abuses women. He is a pig. He will screw up our foreign policy. Trump will come to your house and eat your children!

Instead of placing the focus on Trump, Americans would do better to consider the reasons not to vote for Democrats. If you are white, the Democrats are throwing white

Americans under the bus by accusing them of continued racial oppression of minorities. Unless you are a masochist, don't vote for a party that thinks you are racist, bigoted, sexist, xenophobic, homophobic, and Islamophobic.

If you are non-white, consider two reasons not to vote for Democrats. First, the Democratic Party has spent the last 50 years destroying the meaning of the Civil Rights Act of 1964—which outlawed discrimination on the basis of race, religion, color, sex, and national origin—by making racial categories prevalent in every area of American life and thereby sowing the seeds of division. The potential damage to black people is incalculable. Second, the policies advocated and implemented by Democrats have created the welfare state that traps "people of color" in its hateful web.

"How is it possible that Democrats and progressives can pose as defenders of minorities, the middle class, and the poor?" asks David Horowitz. "Democratic policies have devastated all three." The "Achilles' heel" of the Democratic Party, says Horowitz, is "its monopoly control of the inner cities of America and its responsibility for the misery and suffering inside them. Far from being the party of the people, Democrats and their progressive core represent America's social and cultural elites and constitute the richest, most organized, and most economically powerful political force in American history."

And if you are white, black, brown, yellow, or orange, try to bear in mind that the Democrats are trying to take away your right to free speech, guaranteed by the First Amendment. If the Left has its way, you won't be able to fart without government approval. Many conservatives believe that, despite the best intentions of Donald Trump, the Left has already succeeded in convincing a majority of Americans that the government should run healthcare. Even with the new version of the Affordable Care Act, the federal government has transformed the entire health industry. We are only one step away from a single payer system. Once the federal government obtains total control over our health, it should be easy for the Left to control everything else.

But the most important thing to remember is that if the Left succeeds in its campaign to redistribute income, we will have a country in which half the population is supported by the other half. We are almost there now. If this becomes a reality, the productive half that is doing the supporting—primarily the majority white population—will throw up their hands in disgust. They will be taxed out of existence in order to pay for all the entitlements. The incentive to achieve will disappear, as it has in parts of Europe. "To hell with this," the entrepreneurs will declare. "I'm tired of being a slave for people who refuse to be responsible for themselves." And do you know what they will do? They will pack up and leave. You don't believe me? It is happening right now in France and other European countries as socialist governments ratchet up the tax rates in order to pay for their rapacious nanny states.

When the productive segment of our country moves to Argentina, New Zealand, Singapore, and who knows where else, what will we have left? America will not reward Bernie Sanders by transforming itself into Denmark. No such luck.

America will turn into... Venezuela!!!

Enjoying Our Servitude

Aldous Huxley, author of *Brave New World*, gave a speech in California in 1961 during which he made a prediction:

> *"There will be, in the next generation or so, a pharmacological method of making people love their servitude, and producing dictatorship without tears,*

so to speak, producing a kind of painless concentration camp for entire societies, so that people will in fact have their liberties taken away from them, but will rather enjoy it, because they will be distracted from any desire to rebel by propaganda or brainwashing, or brainwashing enhanced by pharmacological methods."

Can it be that we have already achieved Huxley's prediction? With the common use of recreational drugs and a plethora of material luxuries and adult toys, have we lulled ourselves into the kind of stupor that will facilitate the tyranny of the minority and loss of individual freedoms? Perhaps those of us who argue over Right and Left amount to merely a small fraction of the voting public. Perhaps most Americans don't take the time to worry about who is running the country, and don't really give a damn as long as they have their creature comforts. Perhaps Huxley was right: We have been brainwashed to enjoy our servitude.

Recommended Reading

Brodow, Ed. *Beating the Success Trap: Negotiating Your Own Path to Success.* CreateSpace, 2014.

Brodow, Ed. *In Lies We Trust: How Politicians and the Media Are Deceiving the American Public.* Post Hill Press, 2016.

Brodow, Ed. *Negotiation Boot Camp: How to Resolve Conflict, Satisfy Customers, and Make Better Deals.* CreateSpace, 2014.

Bruce, Tammy. *The New Thought Police: Inside the Left's Assault on Free Speech and Free Minds.* Crown Forum, 2003.

Crowley, Monica. *What the (Bleep) Just Happened? The Happy Warrior's Guide to the Great American Comeback.* Broadside, 2012.

D'Souza, Dinesh. *Obama's America: Unmaking the American Dream.* Regnery, 2012.

Flaherty, Colin. *Don't Make the Black Kids Angry: The Hoax of Black Victimization and How We Enable It.* CreateSpace, 2015.

Geller, Pamela. *The Post-American Presidency: The Obama Administration's War on America.* Threshold Editions, 2010.

Geller, Pamela. *Stop the Islamization of America: A Practical Guide to the Resistance.* WND Books, 2011.
Greer, Scott. *No Campus for White Men: The Transformation of Higher Education into Hateful Indoctrination.* WND Books, 2017.
Hayek, F.A. *The Road to Serfdom.* University of Chicago Press, 2007.
Hitchens, Christopher. *Why Orwell Matters.* Basic Books, 2002.
Horowitz, David. *Big Agenda: President Trump's Plan to Save America.* Humanix Books, 2017.
Levin, Mark R. *Ameritopia: The Unmaking of America.* Threshold Editions, 2012.
Levin, Mark R. *Liberty and Tyranny: A Conservative Manifesto.* Threshold Editions, 2009.
Levin, Mark R. *Plunder and Deceit: Big Government's Exploitation of Young People and the Future.* Threshold Editions, 2015.
Mac Donald, Heather. *The War on Cops: How the New Attack on Law and Order Makes Everyone Less Safe.* Encounter Books, 2016.
Mercer, Ilana. *Into the Cannibal's Pot: Lessons for America from Post-Apartheid South Africa.* Bytech Services, 2012.
Mercer, Ilana. *The Trump Revolution: The Donald's Creative Destruction Deconstructed.* Politically Incorrect Press, 2016.
Murray, Charles. *Coming Apart: The State of White America, 1960-2010.* Crown Forum, 2013.
Orwell, George. *Nineteen Eighty-Four.* Signet Classic, 1961.
Sacks, David O. and Peter Thiel. *The Diversity Myth: Multiculturalism and Political Intolerance on Campus.* Independent Institute, 1998.

Schweizer, Peter. *Clinton Cash: The Untold Story of How and Why Foreign Governments and Businesses Helped Make Bill and Hillary Rich.* Harper, 2016.

Shapiro, Ben. *Bullies: How the Left's Culture of Fear and Intimidation Silences Americans.* Threshold Editions, 2014.

Sowell, Thomas. *Controversial Essays.* Hoover Institution Press, 2002.

Sowell, Thomas. *Wealth, Poverty and Politics: An International Perspective.* Basic Books, 2016.

Steyn, Mark. *America Alone: The End of the World As We Know It.* Regnery, 2006.

Acknowledgments

The author wishes to thank Dr. Fredrick Berke and Fran Wolterding for their editorial acumen and their creative suggestions for improving the manuscript. Don Zirlilight did a great job designing the cover. A. J. Rice has been a priceless marketing resource. The following people were generous with their assistance and moral support: Christopher C. Cayce, Dr. Robert Luthardt, Richard S. Brook, Hon. Joel Blumenfeld, Jeffrey Gitomer, Godfrey Daniel, Chairman Harvey L. Pitt, Theo Androus, Eric Foumberg, Joseph P. Wilson, and Dr. William Launder.

About the Author

Ed Brodow is a political commentator, negotiation expert, and best-selling author of seven books. A nationally recognized television personality, he has appeared on ABC National News, Fox News, PBS, Fortune Business Report, and Inside Edition. Ed is a regular contributor to *Daily Caller* and *Daily Surge*. As the world's top spokesman on the art of negotiation, he has entertained audiences in Paris, Milan, Athens, Singapore, Bangkok, Tokyo, Nairobi, Sao Paulo, Bogota, Montreal, and New York. He is negotiation consultant to some of the world's most prominent organizations, including Microsoft, Goldman Sachs, McKinsey, Learjet, Zurich Insurance, Starbucks, the IRS, and the Pentagon. Ed is a former US Marine Corps officer, Fortune 500 sales executive, and Hollywood movie actor with starring roles opposite Jessica Lange, Ron Howard, and Christopher Reeve. His website is www.brodow.com. If you want to book Ed for a speaking engagement or media appearance, or if you want to cast him in your next movie, email ed@brodow.com.

Made in the USA
Middletown, DE
18 August 2017